John W. Donald

General,

Switgerland

Jens. 1974

PEOPLE : AN INTERNATIONAL CHOICE

The Multilateral Approach to Population

RAFAEL M. SALAS

PEOPLE: AN INTERNATIONAL CHOICE

The Multilateral Approach to Population

by
RAFAEL M. SALAS

PERGAMON PRESS

OXFORD · NEW YORK · TORONTO · SYDNEY · PARIS · FRANKFURT

U.K.	Pergamon Press Ltd., Headington Hill Hall, Oxford, England
U.S.A.	Pergamon Press Inc., Maxwell House, Fairview Park, Elmsford, New York 10523, U.S.A.
CANADA	Pergamon of Canada Ltd., P.O. Box 9600, Don Mills M3C 2T9, Ontario, Canada
AUSTRALIA	Pergamon Press (Aust.) Pty. Ltd., 19a Boundary Street, Rushcutters Bay, N.S.W. 2011, Australia
FRANCE	Pergamon Press SARL, 24 rue des Ecoles, 75240 Paris, Cedex 05, France
WEST GERMANY	Pergamon Press GmbH, 6242 Kronberg/Taunus, Pferdstrasse 1, Frankfurt-am-Main, West Germany

First edition 1976

Library of Congress Catalog Card No. 71-11610

Printed in Great Britain by A. Wheaton & Co., Exeter

Dedication

This book is dedicated to the staff of the United Nations Fund for Population Activities and to the many other people both within and without the United Nations who have contributed to the development of the Fund. Some appear as active participants in the events of this book. Others I have endeavoured to acknowledge in a listing at the end.

Contents

vii

Foreword

It is largely due to the stimulating and sustaining efforts of the United Nations Fund for Population Activities that an international population policy has gradually been evolved, the aims of which can be said to enjoy general approval. It is for this reason that I have great pleasure in writing a foreword to this book by Rafael M. Salas, Executive Director of the United Nations Fund for Population Activities. Under his capable and inspiring direction the Fund has in a short time developed into an international institute that is proving its worth to an ever-increasing extent.

What the Fund has achieved since the end of the sixties is little short of remarkable: some 1400 projects have been developed in nearly 110 countries; it cooperates with approximately 130 governments either as donors or recipients of aid; it maintains a multiplicity of working contacts with nearly all the bodies within the United Nations system and with numerous non-governmental institutions at national and international level; and it has attained a total financial turnover of almost $250 million which, in view of the nature of the Fund's terms of reference and its initially limited political room for manoeuvre, is quite considerable.

What is even more important is the way in which the Fund approaches the world population problem in the conduct of its affairs. Mr. Salas' book deals with this in detail. From its inception, the Fund has shown itself both cautious and wise in handling the delicate aspects which still attach to the problem. Witness, in particular, its understanding of the desirability of primarily national solutions and the need to create a series of alternative provisions designed to deal with the diverse national situations in a technically sound manner. Moreover, the Fund was realistic enough to recognize that a population policy cannot thrive without general social and economic progress.

Only a short time ago during the World Population Conference in Bucharest it became apparent that the principles on which the United Nations Fund for Population Activities had long based its policy and practical aid had become generally accepted and in fact were internationally confirmed in the World Population Plan that was adopted by consensus. Widespread retrospective international recognition, in fact, of the good work which the Fund had done over the years.

Now that general political recognition of the world population problem has been attained, the United Nations Fund for Population Activities can concentrate its energy on translating the consensus into practical measures. The rapid growth of the world population will continue to shape the future for many years to come. But behind this apparently simple demographic fact also lies the terrible prospect of illness and death, poverty, hunger and starvation, illiteracy and unemployment, social upheaval, and economic backwardness.

It is therefore of vital importance to exercise effective influence in the short term on the demographic situation in many countries in conjunction with development programmes. Population programmes can constitute a major prerequisite for the success of development programmes, just as development projects can greatly influence demographic processes.

It is reassuring that interest in organized action concerning the relation between development and population has been so clearly manifested in the applications for aid submitted to the United Nations Fund for Population Activities. But there is another side to the coin. In the first place there is the financial question; applications for aid clearly exceed present financial resources. The Fund will therefore be obliged to define more sharply what the "population activities" which it carries out actually entail. Secondly, the strategic question of how population activities are to be integrated with health care, education, rural development, modernization of agriculture, industrial development, and other economic and social programmes is becoming ever more urgent.

What emerges from this highly readable book is that the Fund has functioned so effectively in the past that it cannot but play an extremely useful role in a new political context.

The Hague   J. P. PRONK
January 1976   *Netherlands Minister for*
                                                              Development Cooperation

Preface

In starting to write this book my mind goes back to an afternoon in July 1969 when I stood outside the departure lounge at Manila Airport waiting for my flight to be called. This was not an ordinary trip. By the very act of departing for New York I was leaving behind me nearly four years in which I had held what was then one of the most influential Cabinet posts in the Philippine Government – that of the Executive Secretary – thus taking, in the Philippine view, a very unusual step. By the same act I was accepting an invitation which Paul G. Hoffman, then Administrator of the United Nations Development Programme, had generously extended to me some months earlier to head a new United Nations action programme in population–later to be named the United Nations Fund for Population Activities (UNFPA).

One reason for making what seemed at that point such a drastic move, was that the possibility of making a contribution in the United Nations to solving what I had begun to think was becoming one of the world's major problems – population – greatly attracted me. Another reason was that I did not believe it was a good thing for an administrator to stay too long in the same job. It is good neither for the administrator nor for the job. I had done the best I could over the past few critical years to help in overall administration of the Philippine Government. The time had come for a change.

After all I had served in the Philippine Government in various capacities for more than a decade including in the latter years being in charge of the management of its Rice Production Campaign. In addition to this public service, my managerial experience had included a period in private enterprise and in the academic community. But I had had no direct exposure to the population discipline. My acquaintance with that field was indirect, through my involvement with food production. Nevertheless the all-pervading influence of the growth, composition and location of population on national progress had been borne in on me from my work with the Philippine National Economic Council and with the Rice Production Programme.

There I had the painful experience of watching at first hand how rapid population growth could wipe out hard-won gains in food production before the benefits could be felt. Hence I was in no doubt as to what uncontrolled increases in numbers meant for families with growing children in terms of food supplies, housing, social services, and employment opportunities.

Indeed, at a time when it is often hard to distinguish the useful from the harmful I felt there were few things so unequivocally important as helping people who wanted such help, to understand and cope with the question of human reproduction both from the point of view of the welfare of the individual and that of the nation as a whole.

From this it was a short step to wanting to know what other countries were doing about their population difficulties and to the start of a personal investigation that led me inevitably to the United Nations.

I had already had some experience of the United Nations. In addition to being my country's representative at meetings of the Economic Commission for Asia and the Far East (ECAFE), the UNDP Governing Council, and the General Assembly, I had served as Vice-President of the International Conference on Human Rights in Teheran in 1968.

While I thought, and still think, that the United Nations was the only possible base from which to launch a worldwide action programme on population, I was aware that the system had liabilities as well as assets. Any United Nations undertaking is, after all, subject to all the conflicts of the international arena. The United Nations is made up of countries of all shapes and sizes, representing the full range of the world's political ideologies, ethical and cultural mores, and political practices. It would have been naïvete itself to think that an action programme in the sensitive field of population could pass smoothly and without setbacks into effective operation.

However, it has always been my policy to tackle the biggest problem first and let the other lesser issues fall into place. The biggest problem, as I saw it at that time, was to devise a means of getting the developed and the developing countries to work together although I knew perfectly well that this would involve the calming of suspicions, the changing of attitudes, and the encouragement of a tremendous generosity of spirit on both sides. For this the Fund would have to mount an acceptable programme of assistance and to assume a leadership role in regard to population matters.

The methods that were used in building up the Fund to serve as an honest broker between two parties and its successes and failures in responding to requests for aid are the subject of this book. I hope it will interest, and perhaps help, those concerned with public sector management, development assistance, and population programmes, or with bettering international relations.

In preparing this book I have been assisted by John Keppel, Ellen M. Ferguson, and Edward S. Trainer. I hope they have enjoyed working with me as much as I have enjoyed working with them. I am also indebted to Bernard Berelson and Richard Gardiner who were kind enough to read the manuscript and to give me the benefit of their helpful criticism and advice.

New York
January 1976

CHAPTER 1

At the Onset

My first appraisal of the United Nations Fund for Population Activities (UNFPA), then a small Trust Fund of the Secretary-General, was far from encouraging. In fact it was difficult not to think in terms of David and Goliath and wonder if this time the tale might have a different ending. On one side was the infant Fund with its limited resources and, on the other, the population problem whose massive proportions were already clearly visible. How the first was to develop the capacity to make any impact on the second was, I suddenly realized, my problem and my assignment.

To appreciate how I felt, it is necessary to look for a moment at how things were in 1969.

World population had reached a new high of over three and a half billion, the last billion having been added over the short period of some thirty years. Faced with this evidence of increasingly rapid population growth, even the complacent began to wonder whether man's seemingly infinite capacity for reproduction was going to outrun the earth's finite capacity to support it. There was little reason to hope for a significant slowdown in the near future. The decline in death rates resulting from medical, technological, and social advances which had given rise to a population upsurge in the Western countries, were now to a growing extent having their effect on the great continents of Africa, Asia, and Latin America where two-thirds of the world's people already lived. Consequently, the demographers were estimating a growth rate in Africa of 2.6 per cent per year, in Asia of 2.1 per cent, and in Latin America of 2.7 per cent, an alarming development whose political, social, and human implications had not yet been fully recognized.

With the exception of India and a few others, the idea that governments can and must do something about the problem came late. I recall that when I was a graduate student in the university some twenty years ago, I and most of my classmates thought that the world was entering a period in which man's extraordinary successes in the development of technology would assure growing abundance. We believed then that most of the injustices and inequalities within and among societies would be progressively reduced. In assuming this we understood demographic data only as part of a given framework within which development programmes must operate.

Very few policy makers and administrators at that time addressed themselves to population problems or planned programmes to deal with them. Population growth was not thought of as a factor that could be consciously changed or directed. In retrospect it is surprising that the idea that population trends could be influenced occurred to so few leaders of countries where population pressures were clearly visible, despite the fact that in such areas policymakers were perennially faced with such questions as How much food do we have to produce this year and how many houses, schools, and clinics do we have to build and maintain under the next Plan?

Yet there was no widespread call for action in population until two interrelated but distinct activities which had been going on since the early years of this century became fused. One was the patient, thorough, descriptive, and analytical work of the scholars in statistics, demography, economics, and other social sciences on population and its relation to the factors of development. The other was the dynamic, pioneering work, largely for humanitarian reasons, of private individuals and organizations in birth control and family planning practices. The interaction between these two activities and their proponents eventually evolved into an assumption that development could and should be accelerated by lessening population growth rates through family planning.

As the acceptance of this view widened, the literature demanding immediate action by governments correspondingly increased in force. In the 1960s the tone became more uncompromising, painting a picture of imminent disaster if nothing was done. With more mathematical sobriety, a highly respected group of scholars from the scientific, educational, and economic fields nevertheless called attention to the possible "limits to growth" and the danger of depletion of resources needed to sustain life.

The United Nations, using the population growth projections of its Population Division, had always taken a moderate view. This had the merit of encouraging action and discouraging fatalism. The United Nations system was slow, however, to move into positive involvement with operational programmes.

My previous exposure to the population problem in my own country had been direct and immediate. It consisted of counting the mouths to be fed from each harvest of the rice crop. My colleagues and I in that food production campaign believed that we were able to devise some successful techniques in managing national food production programmes. I wanted to see if these techniques would work in population on a grander scale.

The Inheritance

It was in this frame of mind that I prepared to take over the direction of my inherited programme of twelve projects, all emanating from the Population Division of the United Nations. The resources, donated by a handful of countries, amounted to some $5 million, of which $3 million had already been obligated, giving me little opportunity for profligacy. The existing programme was limited in scope as well as in size. It consisted in its entirety of fellowship awards for the study of demography and related subjects by the nationals of developing countries and of expert missions on population to a few Asian and African countries. If provision had also been made for supplies and equipment, the whole programme would have fitted neatly and inconspicuously into the accepted mould of United Nations assistance to developing countries. At that time development assistance, almost without variation, involved the transfer of technology, science, and know-how of the industrialized nations to their poorer neighbours.

Although Paul G. Hoffman, the Administrator of the United Nations Development Programme (UNDP), was already pioneering the concept of partnership in development between rich and poor nations, the main flow of assistance still followed traditional lines. It was naturally assumed since the UNFPA came under his supervision that the Fund would conform closely to the procedures of the UNDP. I was pleased to be associated with UNDP which had a well-established and prestigious programme of technical assistance for development. Nevertheless I had some reservations.

My problem was that I did not think the usual patterns of assistance would work.

I had been on the receiving end of international aid programmes in the Philippines, some of which admittedly had advanced economic progress, particularly in agriculture, by many years. But I knew only too well the difficulties involved in deriving full national benefit from even the most generous kinds of externally planned assistance. My experience had shown that it simply was not possible to use external assistance to cure social and economic disorders unless it could be adapted to supplement nationally conceived programmes. The disparities between the structures and technologies of the developed and developing countries were too great. The industrial revolution with its rapid upsurge of technology had come to Europe and North America first and given a head start to countries in these areas. But this technology had been indigenous to them and had not necessarily conferred a universal benefit on others. As many of the earlier aid programmes had demonstrated, too often the technology and organizational forms which had accompanied it had proved difficult for countries of different cultures to digest.

Consequently, I could not see, especially when it came to programmes concerned with the most intimate part of people's lives, how it would be possible to follow patterns under which expertise and methodology suited to one set of countries were transferred directly to another, especially if this process was brought down—as it would have to be—to the family and person to person level.

I was thus thoroughly convinced that the Fund would have to be open to ideas and approaches from all sides and, at all costs, to avoid preconceived formulae. It should not automatically assume that Western technology and Western organization could be applied to situations in developing countries; but it should also not automatically assume that they were inapplicable.

The same rule would have to be brought to bear when it came to methodology deriving from ancient cultures. For who, even today, in West or East can produce a blueprint for man's behavioural patterns and delineate the private aspirations that influence his decisions? In fact I wished it to be clearly recognized by all and sundry that the UNFPA role would be to inform recipient countries on the technology and organizational forms that had been used elsewhere, to respect their choice, and to support the kinds of programmes they wanted to undertake. I went even further on the latter point by insisting that each country work out its own programmes, deriving from and suited to its own particular conditions. In short I felt the existing aid-giving process needed to be reversed.

It is true that with this alternative approach the external aid organization may have rather less control and supervision than when it establishes its own rigid models as a prerequisite for financing. But there are bonuses which far outweigh the disadvantages. By accepting the recipient's proposed programme after reviewing it in the light of his own general mandate, the aid-giver can take part in the decision-making process, understand more fully the problem, and help formulate its solution. He thus assures himself of the usefulness of the operation of which he is a part, makes a real contribution to its success, and safeguards his financial interest in it as far as this is possible. Faith, in this case at least, is not altogether blind.

Furthermore, the aid-giver can see more clearly where injection of additional resources will have the greatest impact. External assistance has from the outset been a small fraction of total development resources, but it can have an effect out of proportion to its size. Like an extra pulley in a block and tackle in the right place, its strength is multiplied.

Another incentive for trying to find new ways of delivering technical assistance stemmed from the rather primitive state of the art in the population field itself. There was very little agreement on how to tackle population factors. New ideas were badly needed. I was also convinced that the time would come when the more affluent nations would encounter population-related problems just as dire and possibly more complex than those facing the developing countries. Thus the giver/receiver concept as it then existed in economic aid programming was hardly likely to prove palatable to the recipient countries, some of which already had more population case histories in hand than the others could amass in a decade of research.

When it came to the general relationship between population and development, there was to my mind even less reason for the Fund to try to conform to the established programming style. Though some aspects of the relationship were clear, many were not. The similarities between the objectives and operations of the Population Fund and those of the UNDP were even more hazy. So why adopt procedures that could easily turn out to be quite wrong for the specific functions which had been assigned to the Fund?

There was one final, potent factor that had to be taken into consideration in defining the UNFPA approach—*time*. Even the most optimistic projections showed a doubling of the earth's inhabitants by the end of the century—as many people again to compete for food, schooling, medical care, housing, jobs—not strangers from another planet but *us*. While ideally each nation with a little assistance should find its own solutions, I was well aware that UNFPA must also seek ways of giving impetus to the process and, if possible, finding shortcuts. As an administrator and cabinet minister from a developing country I knew only too well the extensive amount of time needed to get people to try—let alone accept—new programmes.

Obviously some other concepts had to be found to readjust the balance between donors and recipients and to change current thinking on their relationship. The development of these new concepts, which could only come from straightforward exchanges of information and experiences, called for contributions from both sides as well as from the Fund. Accordingly, it seemed to me essential that the Fund should give an example of candour and frankness in all its dealings. This would also be a way of building credibility in both donor and developing countries. As a result I have always consulted openly, too openly according to some of my colleagues, with representatives of governments, non-governmental organizations, and other agencies.

An episode from my Philippine experience illustrates the importance I place on consultation and candour for winning cooperation and trust.

We were trying to get farmers to accept the new high-yielding strains of rice. The structures through which we had to work were highly complicated and diffused and the instruments of central control were, by the very nature of the exercise, weak. The key lay in the persuasion of a rather large number of people. To accomplish this we had put together what might have seemed an impossibly complex structure: a national production council on which twenty agencies were represented and which was repeated with membership of about ten at the provincial and municipal levels.

By this method, however, every farmer concerned had some say in the matter through his local representative whom he knew and believed in, and was confident that his views were reaching the highest level of government. This made his eventual consent to try the new strains more likely since it was partially the outcome of his own thinking.

In addition to maintaining utmost openness in all operations, I feel a director of any programme channelling assistance from one country to another has a further responsibility—that of building up the confidence of both sides. The donor is inevitably asked to perform an act of trust in the probity of the recipient country and should be helped to realize that the greater the trust the more likely the success of the programmes. The recipient for his part accepts a commitment and should be helped to make honourable use of the assistance for the purpose it is given.

The Fund's First Principles

In 1969, however, the essential element for achieving these technical assistance goals—strong leadership—was still lacking, and this only the Fund could provide.

Here the Fund was faced with plotting a course that made sailing between Scylla and Charybdis look like child's play. If the Fund was to retain the support of its donors it had to take account of their views. If it was to earn the necessary trust of the recipients it had to take account of their views too. Sometimes the two differed widely.

Faced with this dilemma I decided from the start that to be effective the Fund had to be operationally neutral and flexible. By "effective" I meant that the Fund must succeed in making countries conscious of population problems and in stimulating them to undertake national population programmes. By "neutral" I meant strict adherence to and acceptance of population policies as developed by each individual government. I wished to emphasize that in maintaining this approach the Fund in no way backed off from its primary objective of helping to deal with the world's population problems. It merely recognized that in the final issue the solution to these problems depended on the willingness and determination of each and every country to carry out long-term action programmes both on its own account and eventually as part of an international strategy. By "flexible" I meant that the Fund would need as much freedom as possible in the types of programmes it could support, in the kind of assistance it could provide, and in the procedures adopted for delivering such assistance. This was the only way I could devise of responding adequately to the expressed wishes of requesting governments.

But before I could do anything at all, let alone set a course of action, I had to get a general idea of the Fund's proper position as a member of the United Nations family.

Three Constituencies

The United Nations system is a political system whose survival depends on its ability to reflect the complex shifting energies which characterize international politics. Without broad political support a United Nations body, especially one like UNFPA which depends on voluntary contributions, has to be especially nimble in reacting to this environment.

UNFPA has three quite different constituencies within the United Nations system whose support it needs to remain viable and to develop effective programmes: the donors (primarily in the developed world), the recipients (primarily in the developing world), and the organizations carrying out UNFPA-financed programmes. The Fund's initial problems lay in maintaining a balance among the three, as each had divergent ideas on what the Fund should be and how it should operate.

The donors in supporting UNFPA expected it to deal with what they perceived to be the problem of world population growth. They leaned towards fast action aimed directly at reducing growth rates. The recipients, on the other hand, with their quite different cultural orientations and their pressing short-range problems, often did not see the reduction of their population growth as a high priority. In addition, they were basically resistant to definitions of problems, and strategies for dealing with them, which had originated in the developed world. Even from the start they tended, for obvious reasons, to be less interested than the donors in detailed plans for programmes supported by outsiders, and they pressed for a flexible definition of the kinds of programmes which might be legitimately funded under the name of population.

Then there were the United Nations Secretariat, the regional economic commissions, and the specialized organizations in the system. Over the years these highly varied and quite autonomous organizations had built up special relations with individual governments and held positions of considerable influence and power, both nationally and internationally, in their areas of competence. Not only the United Nations proper but also the International Labour Organization (ILO), the Food and Agriculture Organization (FAO), the United Nations Educational, Scientific and Cultural Organization (UNESCO), the World Health Organization (WHO), and the United Nations Children's Fund (UNICEF) already had limited population elements within their regular programmes. So it was understandable that they tended to see the Fund as a welcome source of supplementary financing to develop population programmes within their respective spheres.

It was less credible that I saw the Fund as an entity which could be developed into the main operational arm of the United Nations system in population, bringing together all these scattered programmes into a unified effort with the Fund in the leadership role. The odds were in favour of the Fund becoming no more than a useful appendage of the established organizations. But in my view, then and now, that would have been the end of any effective involvement by the United Nations system in population matters and of any chance of achieving an international strategy.

Doubtless many well-intentioned colleagues in the United Nations felt that my aims for the Fund were over-ambitious. On the face of it I was a newcomer heading up a small unit which could only survive and launch a competent programme if it had the support and cooperation of the very organizations it was about to challenge for the leadership role in all population programmes within the United Nations and, when feasible, outside as well.

Fortunately, events overtook the issue before it could develop. In a remarkably short time the Fund was strengthened by a high influx of contributions and was able to generate plans for population work to which the United Nations organizations had to conform in order to share in the financial allocations.

Not surprisingly, collaboration with these organizations proved to be among the greatest assets the Fund was to have in that they gave the Fund status, roots, and contacts that would otherwise have had to be built from the start by the new unit. They also gave the Fund access to their special constituencies, thus making it easier to add population elements to government programmes. In many cases these supplementary projects were the introductory phase for more comprehensive population plans.

It was true that there was some self-interest in the organizations encouragement of the Fund in that the resources that became available enabled them to broaden their programmes. But I think the reciprocal arrangements have worked very well for both. Though I will admit in the process I learned one lesson, that is in the international world the person who pays the piper cannot always call the tune.

The next hurdle I foresaw was acclimatization to the United Nations bureaucracy. Because the United Nations is a multinational system, power is diffuse even in its secretariats. The member nations are the governors and often look over the shoulder of the Secretary-General, as well as those of the heads of agencies or programmes, to see what is happening in regard to internal administration and staff, particularly matters concerning their own nationals. The character of United Nations organizations is thus very different from that of an army or the Church or, to a lesser extent, a national bureaucracy, where the leader has sanctions at his disposal. Of the principal sorts of inducement usually available to a leader such as physical force, money, and granting of political patronage or social status, only the status incentive is really available in the United Nations system.

Political skills are thus at a premium. The support of a wide range of countries must be won in order to guarantee the success of any operation, let alone ensure a solid backing when controversial issues arise on which a director has to take a stand. Woe to the director who in his own establishment does not remember that the members of his multicultural staff have also emerged from the same variety of backgrounds and, even as international civil servants, bring with them some stamp of their national origins.

Inevitably, the diverse nature of the United Nations calls for a rather fluid approach to gaining support for a course of action. For example, if an executive officer was from the beginning to come in with a programme unilaterally worked out in detail, because of the different perceptions of the various member governments, and internally of the various staff members, virtually every aspect of his programme would meet with some objections. In this way he would have generated far more opposition than support. The idea is to find the elements on which agreement can be reached, and then to build a workable arrangement on that basis, while in the process keeping the main objective clearly in view. I think all United Nations executive officers learn this lesson very fast and then devise their own methods of procedure. I shall describe mine later.

Despite these complexities, I did not expect to encounter any insurmountable obstacles to the carrying out of a dynamic and even radical population action programme within the United Nations system. Though in effect the Fund was blessed with a board of governors of 130 (now 147) member states, a disquieting prospect for any chief executive, many of these countries were already backers of the new action programme and the others were, hopefully, future participants. And even at the early stage, I felt universal participation should be the major UNFPA goal. This explains many of the small, and apparently disparate, projects we funded over the years to encourage hesitant governments.

In addition, the United Nations customary approach to controversy of trying for negotiation and cooling-off periods rather than of pressing for decisions when tempers are running high, seemed to me the only possible climate in which to work out programmes in the population field. Therefore, conforming to the rules and regulations of an international bureaucracy was a small price to pay to get a world wide programme under way.

It is not too much to claim, at this point, that the policy of candour in all our dealings and the programming principles of neutrality and flexibility have had beneficial effects on all three of the Fund's constituencies. Over six operational years, the Fund's donors have steadily increased their contributions, grown in number and tabled no serious complaints on the many formal and informal occasions on which I have met with them. The recipients have also grown in numbers, widened their population programmes and strengthened their political support of the Fund. The agencies and organizations helping to implement the programmes have established close working relationships with both the countries and the Fund and developed new expertise to meet the challenges of untried and innovative programmes.

CHAPTER 2

In the United Nations

I arrived in New York in July 1969 without a scrap of paper to show that I was going to work for the United Nations. The post which Mr. Hoffman had invited me to take did not formally exist. The exchanges with Mr. Hoffman had been oral. So, here I was, in New York, with only his word that there was a task to be done and that I was the man to do it. But Hoffman's word was as good as his bond: the job was officially created and I was appointed.

It took about a week to sort things out. At UNDP Headquarters in the Alcoa Building in the United Nations Plaza I was lent the office of one of Hoffman's assistants, then on leave, and allowed to share a secretary. A little later I was given miniscule staff—one professional and three clerks—and office space of our own in the same building. I remember being shown my office by my one professional officer who was pleased at our getting any space at all which would allow the unit to be together. I will admit that my own reaction was at best mixed. The office was 14 feet deep and 9 feet wide, with one window giving on to an interior and uninteresting court. The space was being sublet from the African-American Institute, and directly outside my door was an open alcove containing two burners on which Institute personnel would make hamburgers or warm up cans of spaghetti.

Despite efforts to take things as they came, I could not help contrasting my circumstances with the large and handsome office in the Malacañang Palace with its elegant chandeliers and beautiful furnishings which I had relinquished.

But logic came to my aid. An organization begins with three. I had two more than that. I was being tested. It was up to me to provide the skill and determination needed to build this embryonic unit into an effective force.

There was also the matter of my rank. I was not familiar with the grading system in the United Nations before I came. I simply assumed that the status given was equal to the job. In a very short while I realized that the top grade of the directorial level was not enough when one negotiates with government ministers and heads of various agencies and organizations within the system. Evidently I had not only to set the pace but make the grade as well.

This was achieved in under four years. Strangely enough, in my particular case, I detected a positive correlation between my grade and the Fund's resources. In 1970 it took a Director to administer a $20 million kitty. In 1971 the jump in resources to a cumulative level of $48 million called for the greater wisdom and acuity of an Assistant Secretary-General. In 1973 with assured contributions totalling over $120 million, the assignment immediately required the still more elevated services of an Under Secretary-General, a rank only one step below that of the Secretary-General of the United Nations.

The credit for this sequence of events, which gave operational strength to the Fund and peace of mind and negotiating clout to me, is also due to two Secretaries-General of the United Nations (U Thant and Kurt Waldheim), two Administrators of the UNDP (Paul Hoffman and Rudolph Peterson), many other supporters in the United Nations system, and a considerable number of government representatives from donor and recipient countries.

My first act was to learn as much as I could about the situation facing me. I read everything I could lay my hands on, particularly books by people engaged in various aspects of population. Bernard Berelson, then President of the Population Council, was one of the first to be approached. In response to my request for reading material he provided me with a small library, the nucleus of the well-stocked shelves of reference books UNFPA now has. My initial discussions with Berelson were most instructive, particularly regarding the potentialities and problems of family planning, and helped me develop the guidelines under which the Fund still operates.

I also called on everybody whom I could find in and out of the United Nations system to become acquainted with the points of view of the individual member governments and organizations and to inform them of the existence of a United Nations Fund for Population Activities. I visited on foot or by car, bus, and subway, every chief of the permanent missions to the United Nations who would receive me, and that totalled 108. Judging from the appearance of my shoes afterwards, that must have been a record.

My calls were usually, but not always, welcomed. One ambassador told me: "You come from the Philippines, a good country, and are, no doubt, a good man; sit on my sofa, drink my coffee, but don't even try to talk to me about population." Another was always somewhere else when I sought to arrange a time for my call: the envoy of a 99 per cent Catholic country, he obviously suspected my motives. I do not, however, give up easily. A little later, on a trip to his country, with the help of the UNDP Resident Representative, I was able to explain to the Government and the Church that UNFPA was neutral in respect to policy and was prepared to respond to requests for assistance with demographic data gathering as well as family planning. It was also helping Catholic programmes, and in Africa was assisting one study on how to overcome sterility and subfertility. This country later gave the Fund a modest but very welcome contribution.

Early Programmes

Inevitably, the United Nations involvement with population prior to my arrival was the foundation on which Fund programmes had to be built.[1]

Despite the attempts in the early fifties of farsighted people such as Julian Huxley, the first Director-General of UNESCO and B. R. Sen, then the Director-General of the Food and Agriculture Organization of the United Nations (FAO), little attention was paid to population matters except by demographers and scholars such as David Glass, Alfred Sauvy, Kingsley Davis, and W. D. Borrie. Huxley's first call of alarm in 1948 that "Somehow or other population must be balanced against resources or civilization will perish" went practically unnoticed.[2] B. R. Sen was also talking in the wilderness when he warned the 1965 FAO Conference that

---

[1] An excellent account of the early history of population activities is given in Richard Symonds and Michael Carder, *The United Nations and the Population Question: 1945-1970*, McGraw-Hill, New York, 1973.

[2] Symonds, pp. 53-54.

"Food and agriculture is no longer growing faster than population in any of the developing regions. On the contrary, food production has been lagging behind population growth. ... The efforts, often heroic, of the developing countries combined with aid in all forms channelled through numerous multilateral and bilateral sources have not so far proved sufficient to reverse this dangerous trend."[3]

"Heroic work" in population was begun by a few private organizations and government development assistance agencies in the 1950s. In 1952 two private agencies concerned with assistance to international population activities were established: the International Planned Parenthood Federation (IPPF) and the Population Council.

The IPPF became the umbrella organization for private agencies offering family planning services in most of the developing countries, and has thus played a crucial role in stimulating government family planning programmes and generating public support for them. Under the imaginative and active direction of, first, the late Sir David Owen, formerly Co-Administrator of the UNDP, and then of Julia Henderson, formerly Head of both the United Nations Bureau of Social Affairs and the Office of Technical Cooperation Operations, IPPF forged strong links with the United Nations system and has continued to provide important support to national programmes and to sponsor relevant global research and development activities.

The Population Council, founded by John D. Rockefeller 3rd and very ably led by Frank Notestein and then Bernard Berelson, has provided substantive leadership in the population field. It, along with the Ford and Rockefeller Foundations, has helped to develop institutional capacity to study population problems and train experts; to design, undertake, and publicize pilot projects; to survey knowledge, attitudes, and practices in regard to family planning among potential recipients; and to consult with governments on the design of national family planning programmes.

Bilateral government assistance in population was pioneered in 1958 when Sweden helped initiate an experimental programme in Sri Lanka. Sweden was soon joined by the United Kingdom, the United States, other northern European countries, and Canada.

Stimulus was also given to the population movement by a book which came out in 1958 entitled *Population Growth and Economic Development*

[3] Symonds, pp. 127-32.

in Low-income Countries. This was a systematic and authoritative study of the economic implications of different rates of population growth in India by the demographer Ansley Coale and the economist Edgar Hoover.

Despite these various activities, international assistance in population amounted to only about $2 million in 1960 and $18 million in 1965. Large-scale government action did not come until the late 1960s.

Although there had been a small pilot study on the voluntary limitation of families in India carried out under WHO auspices in the early 1950s, a study which was not viewed kindly by the WHO governing body, the key event which opened the door for the development of a United Nations system action programme did not come until 1966. Then the General Assembly unanimously passed a resolution entitled "Population Growth and Economic Development" calling upon the United Nations system "to assist, when requested, in further developing and strengthening national and regional facilities for training, research, information and advisory services in the field of population, bearing in mind the different character of population problems in each country and region and the needs arising therefrom."[4]

With the legislative light now green, the United Nations Department of Economic and Social Affairs (ESA) in the United Nations Secretariat made plans to intensify its work in the field of population. Up to this point, ESA population activities had consisted primarily of the standardization, publication, and analysis of demographic statistics. The move towards action programmes was a radical step by no means welcomed by all. It was, for instance, mistrusted by some who opposed the expansion into areas beyond the clearly defined disciplines of demography. What is more, funds were tight and this would obviously call for extra budgetary financing which many doubted would be forthcoming. The latter was a miscalculation.

After much discussion within the Secretariat and with certain industrialized countries, notably Sweden and the United States, in July of 1967 the Secretary-General, U Thant, announced the creation of a special Trust Fund for Population Activities to supplement the regular United Nations budgetary appropriation. Member states were invited to contribute to it.

In taking this action, U Thant was not merely acting as the head of a

[4] General Assembly Resolution 2211 (XXI) (17 December 1966).

great organization approving the suggestion of one of his subordinate branches. He was worried about the implications of population trends for the welfare of men and women around the world, their children, and their descendants, and was willing to put his personal prestige on the line and to take any constructive step open to him. While well aware that his popularity as Secretary-General would not be enhanced in many quarters, he went on record saying: "The most urgent conflict confronting the world today is not between nations or ideologies, but between the pace of growth of the human race and the insufficient increase in resources needed to support mankind in peace, prosperity and dignity."

Despite the fact that the General Assembly's resolution permitting an action programme in population had been passed unanimously, many countries still had reservations. These would have come into play if the assessed contributions to the United Nations and the Specialized Agencies were to be affected. There would have been similar objections in the use of UNDP funds for family planning. Although contributions to UNDP were voluntary, its donors included a number of countries which on ideological grounds were pretty certain to object.

As evidence of this kind of opposition, I cite the voting on the draft Declaration on Social Progress and Development[5] which took place in the Third Committee of the General Assembly in 1969. Some objected to the suggestion that couples should have not only the knowledge but also the means to enable them to decide on the number and spacing of their children. That in a separate vote on the inclusion of the words "and means" more than a third of the delegates present either voted no or abstained shows the extent of these objections.

It is germane to the story to recall that the primary functions of the United Nations, at the time it was set up at the end of World War II, related to political and security matters. The main function of its Secretariat and its various departments, commissions, and divisions was to staff its various legislative bodies. The Specialized Agencies are administratively separate from the United Nations proper. Some of them, such as ILO and the Universal Postal Union, antedated the United Nations. They were created to act as international forums and to set standards for various fields like health, education, science, agriculture, and labour.

Technical assistance for economic and social programmes in developing

[5] General Assembly Resolution 2524 (XXIV) (11 December 1969).

countries was a relatively new venture. It began early in the 1950s with voluntary contributions from governments especially earmarked to expand the advisory capacities and services of the Agencies. The UNDP now administers most of these funds which are not included in the regular budgets of the United Nations and the Specialized Agencies.

Administratively, U Thant's action in setting up a population Trust Fund under his direct authority had several advantages. The Trust Fund had no intergovernmental governing body and thus was not buffeted by attacks from the unconvinced during its formative period. In addition, calls on its resources did not compete with demands being made on the already overcommitted regular budgets of the United Nations and Specialized Agencies and the UNDP resources earmarked for economic and social assistance. Money, however, was not all that was at stake. United Nations organizations had been formed to administer, and had become accustomed to administering, older and by now well-established programmes. They were very busy with these activities and could not be expected to have either much time or sympathy for a programme like population.

In its initial phase, and before it became the UNFPA, the Trust Fund for Population was intended to finance population work within the United Nations Secretariat. It was estimated that the modest sum of $5.5 million would be a sufficient supplement to the regular budget over a five-year period. These funds were to be used to build up staff resources at United Nations headquarters and in the regional economic commissions.

Efforts to Become Operational

Much of the burden of making something out of the new Fund fell at that time to Milos Maçura, a Yugoslav demographer who directed the United Nations Population Division in the Department of Economic and Social Affairs. During the period 1967 to 1969 Maçura laid the groundwork within the United Nations Secretariat for an expanded population programme. Maçura, Leon Tabah (the French demographer who now heads the Division), and the other able men and women who have worked there deserve recognition for the very substantial and fundamental contribution they have made.

Though a relatively small body of people, they have forwarded expert knowledge throughout the world on a wide range of demographic topics through research, discussion, publication, and assistance to others, and by these means at the same time have laid the necessary groundwork for government awareness of population factors. The Division's periodic projections of global trends and its publications, such as *The Determinants and Consequences of Population Trends*, first published in 1953, constitute milestones in the slow progress of the world to consciousness of the emerging situation.

It was from Maçura that I learned firsthand the difficulties of running a programme within the United Nations system. And his insights into the workings of the various groups of specialists in the population field were my maps for seeing my way through many problems.

Maçura worked under Philippe de Seynes, the Under Secretary-General for Economic and Social Affairs. Both he and I profited from our contacts with this learned man. I met de Seynes a few weeks after my arrival in New York but I really did not know him until we had had a number of informal luncheons usually with delectable French cuisine. It was in this ambiance and undistracted by any office problems that we discussed his views on development, population, and United Nations affairs. These were the most instructive sessions I have had with anyone in our business because de Seynes not only had a profound academic knowledge of these subjects but also a breadth of understanding which far exceeded that of most of his contemporaries.

The approach to developing an operational programme at that time was to build up a United Nations field staff called Population Programme Officers (PPOs) to help countries prepare population projects for funding. The original *aide-mémoire* announcing the creation of the Trust Fund stated that the work of the PPOs in the elaboration of detailed regional programmes and the drawing up of regional and country projects should be carried out in 1967 and 1968 and termed it "the most critical element of the whole programme, on which the future expansion of United Nations activities in the field of population will largely depend".

Because of the complicated procedures in international recruitment of experts, the first PPOs did not complete their training and arrive at their posts until February 1969. The delay in getting an action programme launched in the field, coupled with the vagueness surrounding the role and jurisdiction of the Specialized Agencies, was a source of increasing dissatisfaction to the donors. Finally, several governments decided to request U Thant to transfer the administration of the Trust Fund to Paul Hoffman of the UNDP. Events leading to this provide some insight into how decisions are made in the system.

Aware that pressure for urgent action was mounting, in 1968 the Population Division hired a consultant, Richard Symonds, at that time with the Institute of Development Studies of the University of Sussex, to undertake a study "On the ways in which the new Trust Fund could best be developed as a flexible operational arm of the United Nations programme in population".[6] In a way his report was like a shot of adrenalin. It significantly raised the sights of the Secretariat on the possible size, scope, and influence of the United Nations involvement in population.

The report recommended that the Fund be expanded to support programmes of the Specialized Agencies and UNICEF, in addition to those of the United Nations proper, at an annual level of $5 million in the first year, $10 million in the second, and $20 million in the third. It said that the Fund should finance not only technical assistance but also research, transport, and equipment. The Fund should be more flexible than other United Nations system technical assistance programmes in financing local costs and in using local institutions to carry out research. While not rejecting the ultimate establishment of a United Nations Population Agency, the report proposed as an immediate measure the appointment of a United Nations Commissioner for Population Programmes who would coordinate the programme and whose status would enable him to attend meetings of the very high level Administrative Committee on Coordination which brings together the heads of all the organizations of the United Nations system.

Many of the suggestions in this report were eventually used in UNFPA's first directive to Resident Representatives on its procedures and operation in 1969. But its effect in 1968 was to point out to countries the scope of the action required and the need for an authoritative head of the programme.

At about this time the United States, following the lead of Denmark,

[6] Report on the United Nations Trust Fund for Population Activities and the role of the United Nations in Population Action Programmes (September, 1968).

became the second and largest donor to the Trust Fund with a contribution of $1 million. It was committed to seeing fast action in population. Internally, within the United States, this view found support in an authoritative and thoughtful United States/United Nations Association panel report under the chairmanship of John D. Rockefeller 3rd entitled "World Population—a Challenge to the United Nations and its System of Agencies".

This particular report, well received inside the US Government, recommended that a Population Commissioner be appointed within UNDP and not in the United Nations Secretariat. The report foresaw the need for expansion of the Fund rapidly up to an annual rate of $100 million per year. The United States had always considered UNDP as the best channel for assistance funds of this magnitude. It was consistent with this position that John McDonald of the US State Department made a statement in the United Nations Economic and Social Council to the effect that the next US contribution for population would be made to UNDP in order to get some action.

Transfer of the Fund

U Thant transferred the administration of the Trust Fund to UNDP in May, 1969. Undoubtedly, a sharply expanded interest in population helped enormously in getting the Fund through its first uncertain months of existence. But the transfer to UNDP gave it the initial thrust.

There were several good reasons why this move had the hearty support of donors, recipients, and agencies. In the first place Hoffman had proved to be a very effective fundraiser for UNDP. It was hoped he could do the same for the Fund. Then UNDP was a financial and managerial operation which had functioned by entrusting project implementation to other United Nations organizations and therefore was not in competition with them. The Fund could be expected to adopt the same procedures. Moreover, UNDP was well known for its partnership policy under which UNDP, the agencies and the recipient governments were considered as partners in the joint enterprise of development. That the Fund should proceed along the same lines was taken as a foregone conclusion. In addition, UNDP had a good reputation for its ability to work in harmony with the United Nations organizations. This was an important aspect from the point of view of the donors who were concerned with the need for an authoritative centre of leadership in population and were confident that UNDP could provide the unifying process.

Finally, population assistance had to be an integral part of other development assistance if it was to be acceptable to recipient countries. For instance, when developing countries could see that family planning would help other efforts to improve the health and education of children, they would be more likely to accept and promote national population programmes. UNDP was the mechanism by which this close coordination between population and other programmes might be achieved.

The transfer looked fine on paper. But when it came to taking over the direction of the Fund a few months later I found with distinct shock that full control over the resources of the Fund had not been clearly and unequivocally vested in UNDP.

Officials in the United Nations had initially been cautious about broadening the United Nations system effort into a major action programme, and had been slow to prepare for more operational activities. Subsequently, however, they saw the possibilities of the programme and became reluctant to have responsibility for its leadership transferred away from them to UNDP.

In negotiations between the United Nations and UNDP it had, I discovered, been agreed that despite responsibility for the administration of the Fund having been transferred to UNDP, responsibility for the technical appraisal of projects was to be retained by the Department of Economic and Social Affairs. It had also been agreed to allow the United Nations Controller, who was the custodian of UNFPA as well as UNDP money, to withdraw part of the Fund's resources for use by the United Nations to cover central costs before making them available to UNFPA for allocation to purposes of its choice.

I had been invited to take charge of the programme but it was obvious that my control of its resources was minimal.

There were other problems. The operating arm at UNDP Headquarters at that time was the Bureau of Operations and Programming. In anticipation of the transfer of the Fund, a small unit had been set up within it to deal with population matters. When I arrived this unit was not placed under me. It was thus far from clear how I could discharge the responsibilities I was supposed to assume as part of this quadripartite administration.

Both the Symonds and the US/UNA reports had recommended that there should be a Commissioner for Population. However, counter-pressures on the part of other United Nations organizations made it untenable to appoint someone to lord it over the whole system; and after such discussion the very modest title of director was decided upon.

My review of the situation thus disclosed: considerable progress in laying the foundations for United Nations participation in population matters but considerable disagreement and little action on constructing the programme; strong, even vociferous, support from some member states of the United Nations and often, less than silent reservations on the part of others; thoughtful suggestions as to the kind of programme the Fund should undertake, but confused and inconsistent delineation of authority and responsibility for bringing the programme into being. In fact, I was in the curious position of knowing where we were going but not knowing how we were going to get there.

CHAPTER 3

First Steps

As a result of my early talks with U Thant, Paul Hoffman, C. V. Narasimhan (who at that time was serving both as *Chef de Cabinet* to U Thant and as Deputy Administrator to Hoffman), Philippe de Seynes, and others, I concluded they wanted to see what I could do. I reflected that it was not too unusual to leave a new boy alone for a while to see how he would act. So I made a list of what I needed to get the Fund under way.

First, I had to have almost immediately at least a minimal staff to extend my own capabilities and to start preparatory activities.

Second, I had to bring about re-negotiation of the arrangements concerning the Fund between UNDP and the United Nations and to establish UNFPA's full authority over all the monies in or coming to the Fund.

Third, I had to draw up a programme and to establish my authority to begin activities.

Fourth, with Hoffman's help, I had to get much-expanded fundraising activities under way.

Fifth, I had to solicit the help of the various organizations with which the Fund would have to deal inside and outside the United Nations system and to involve them in the Fund's affairs. On the one hand, UNFPA would really need their help and counsel; and, on the other, it could not afford their misunderstanding or resentment, particularly in its then embryonic state.

Staff Recruitment

There were two places to look for ready-made staff: the small unit within the Bureau of Operations and Programming which UNDP had set up to help with Fund affairs, and the Population Programmes and Projects Office (PPPO) which the United Nations Population Division had founded when it expected to continue to administer the Fund.

My first UNFPA colleague was an American named John Keppel who had been recruited to take charge of the UNDP unit. A vigorous New Yorker, Keppel had an interesting background which included a degree in the history of fine arts and a fellowship in international relations, both from Harvard. He had also studied population at Johns Hopkins University. Before coming to the UNDP in 1969 he had served in his country's foreign service. I need hardly say the Fund was inordinately lucky to have as one of its earliest staff members a man who was both informed on population and versed in international relations.

I had barely assumed my own duties when Keppel concluded that his unit should be released from the Bureau of Operations and Programming and put under me. On his own initiative he entered into negotiations with Myer Cohen, Assistant Administrator, to bring this about. Fortunately, both the Symonds and the Rockefeller reports had called for an autonomous unit to be set up within UNDP to administer UNFPA. Even more fortunately, Myer Cohen himself thought that this was the right thing to do. There were, therefore, no objections to my receiving delegated authority from Hoffman over the Fund's affairs and getting the tiny unit as my initial staff.

Keppel immediately proposed that we explore the staff potentialities of the other possible source–the PPPO.

Here we succeeded in persuading Halvor Gille, Associate Director of the Population Division and chief of the PPPO, that we needed him in the Fund. Gille, an economist from the University of Copenhagen, worked for some years with the Swedish and Danish governments and also undertook a research programme at the London School of Economics. Since 1950 he had been associated with the United Nations Social Affairs and Population Divisions and, apart from a short spell with the Danish Social Research Institute in Copenhagen, had held a number of key posts in these Divisions in New York, Bangkok, and Geneva. Getting Gille transferred to the Fund to serve as Deputy Executive Director was politically important. It also gave the Fund an experienced population specialist.

I wanted, as far as possible, to assemble a young and vigorous staff who would above all be receptive to new ideas. In the Philippines, in managing the rather large number of people under my direct control and the larger mass of the civil service, I relied much on a group of young people who could work well both on the administrative and the political sides. The former were structured situations where there were explicit rules of conduct and superior-subordinate relationships; the latter, unstructured situations where the people with whom they were to deal were in no way under their control and thus where persuasive skills were the first requisite. Many of these young people have gone on to hold important positions in the Philippine Government today.

Soon after I came to New York I met two UNDP officers who were considered "Young Turks". As I liked their sort of energy I asked them to join as programme officers. At the same time, to answer my need for a Special Assistant with political experience in the United Nations system, a former acting head of a United Nations Mission was recommended to me and soon joined the Fund. Thus, within six months we had the nucleus of what has proved to be a very effective staff.

The Fund and the United Nations

Basically little could be done until the relationship with the United Nations Secretariat had been adjusted. We recommended to Hoffman that the agreement under which the Fund was administered should be changed in two important ways: firstly, the Administrator of UNDP should be given clear responsibility for decision making with regard to all expenditures of monies given to the Fund whether these were for administrative backstopping or programme operations; and, secondly, the provision setting up the Department of Economic and Social Affairs as the sole coordinator of expert opinion should be revoked, thus leaving the Administrator and the Fund free to deal directly with major elements of the United Nations family and other appropriate institutions as they might choose.

Hoffman was quick to see that unless these actions were taken and the Fund's authority in regard to the Specialized Agencies and other elements of the United Nations system established, undoubtedly contributions for population purposes would go directly to the Specialized Agencies. What would be worse, the whole idea of creating a single point of coordination within the United Nations system for population programmes would be jeopardized, not to mention the donors' interest in expanding the population work of the United Nations system.

Both Sweden and the United States had already made a number of contributions for population work directly to Specialized Agencies. Hence the danger of diverse channelling of population funds was very real.

Hoffman discussed these questions with de Seynes and also suggested, as we had urged him to do, that the field officers of the United Nations Population Division, the Population Programme Officers (PPOs), be transferred to UNFPA.

After much more discussion, a compromise was reached generally along the lines suggested but leaving the PPOs under the control of the Population Division while, theoretically operating under my direction on Fund matters. This divided responsibility for the field staff not surprisingly turned out to be unworkable and a bone of contention between the Population Division and the Fund over a period of two years until the PPO programme was finally phased out and its work taken over by UNFPA Coordinators.

Establishing the Fund's Programme

Before Halvor Gille left the Department of Economic and Social Affairs he had started what turned out to be a long series of consultations among the United Nations organizations as to how the system could help in the population field and what each agency could do. When he joined us, Gille continued to act as the moving force of these efforts. Eventually the results of these consultations were embodied in the book put out by the Department in January 1971, *Human Fertility and National Development: A Challenge to Science and Technology*. In a more immediate sense, however, they served to define the substantive aspects of the programmes in the United Nations system. They were the blueprint on the basis of which we sought expanded resources. As such, they were the precursor of the present annually revised UNFPA Work Plan.

Even the bare recitation of the headings and subheadings of the five-year programme outlined in this book showed the scope of what was conceived: An International Strategy on Population; Statistics (census operations, vital and health statistics); Research (human reproductive biology and contraceptive techniques, population growth and development, attitude studies, health and welfare aspects of family planning, organization and evaluation of programmes, social policy research); Training (manpower requirements, promotion of training activities, development of professional training, short-term training, regional centres, fellowships and stipends, international interdisciplinary training schemes); Communications (involvement of existing programmes and personnel, teaching at schools and training centres, development of teaching methods and materials, mass media, information services); Field Projects (advisory services, demonstration and pilot projects, *post-partum* programmes, financial assistance for data collection); Conferences and Seminars.

While we were thinking through the substance of the Fund's programme, members of the United Nations system were clarifying their own interests in the field of population. Briefly described, they were as follows:

United Nations (Department of Economic and Social Affairs)	demography and statistics; demographic research and projections; population policy; economic, social, and administrative aspects of population programmes.
ILO	education and motivation of workers; family planning in occupational health services; population and employment.
FAO	education and motivation among rural population and agricultural development.
UNESCO	population education; family planning support communication; social science research.
WHO	family planning in health services; human reproduction research; health aspects of population dynamics.
UNICEF	equipment, vehicles, and supplies; population training inputs to field programmes affecting mothers and children.

UNFPA's Principles and Procedures

To get going we needed an authoritative statement of UNFPA principles and procedures under which headquarters staff, Resident Representatives directing UNDP Field Offices, and the various United Nations Agencies could start operations. It was also necessary to obtain the comments of governments and United Nations organizations so they would feel some commitment toward them when they were finalized. We thought the best way to accomplish this would be in two stages: a short interim statement to let the United Nations system start moving followed by a fuller one to serve as the basis for consultations with governments, agencies, and other interested organizations.

Using, in part, material from the Symonds Report but also taking into account UNDP practice and experience, we quickly produced two texts, a circular letter to the Resident Representatives signed by the Administrator and an extended draft statement of the Fund's Principles and Procedures. Both included large elements of innovation in respect to traditional United Nations patterns. I shall not here distinguish between the two since to a large extent they overlap, but will mention a few of the key points in them.

The autonomous character of UNFPA was provided for by establishing that the Administrator of UNDP would be assisted by an UNFPA Advisory Board and would nominate a Director of the Fund who would have his own staff. I shall return to the Advisory Board later. It was important that the Director should have his own staff through which he could administer the Fund rather than being merely advisory to the Administrator. Obviously a separate unit with a high degree of operational freedom was essential if a programme was to be developed vigorously and quickly, if donors were to be convinced that the matter was being handled seriously, if the lessons already learned by others in the population field were to be mastered, and if adequate coordination with other organizations providing assistance with population programmes was to be maintained.

A second important decision was to make the UNDP Resident Representatives the field representatives of the Fund and to provide that they be assisted by the PPOs. The reasons were plain. The Resident Representatives act as the coordinating centre for all assistance programmes in the country of their assignment. Accordingly they maintain contact at the highest level in the governments to which they are accredited, and not merely with the heads of departments as is usually the case with the field representatives of the Specialized Agencies. Effective population programmes would be interdisciplinary and interdepartmental in nature, and hence should be coordinated and supported by the central authorities. To permit the Agencies to work independently in each country would increase the fragmentation already brought about by the departmental structure of governments. It would, moreover, be important for recipient governments to feel that UNFPA-supported programmes were truly theirs and not just something of interest to one or another United Nations organization and to which one of their government departments had acquiesced.

In regard to the implementation of projects, the Principles and Procedures draft paper said that while "the Administrator will normally choose the participating and executing agency for a project from among the United Nations or Agencies related to it", he might "choose an agency outside the United Nations system if it seems advisable to do so". This was a radical but necessary departure from existing United Nations practices. There were several sound reasons for this provision. Many private organizations and institutions had initiated population programmes during the period when governments were reluctant to do so. Their programmes had, in most cases, received if not official at least tacit government approval. It seemed wise to leave the door open to being able to respond to requests for assistance from national private organizations or to use an international private organization as an executing agency. There were instances where governments were more than happy to have the local family planning organizations conduct family planning programmes, and on occasions were willing to let them use the facilities of government hospitals in the process, but did not want to take the official responsibility for such activities.

In addition, while the Fund meant to do most of its business through the members of the United Nations system, it would be a challenge for these organizations to know that when they were encountering difficulties in the delivery of assistance there were other organizations ready and willing to do the job. We did in fact very early in our operations fund some activities through the IPPF and later through many other private organizations.

This was an important divergence from UNDP practice at that time, under which all projects were executed on UNDP's behalf by the various United Nations offices and the Specialized Agencies. Had we accepted the principle that only United Nations organizations could execute projects, it would have meant that the Agencies and not the recipient countries would have had the stronger voice in determining the nature of requests to the Fund.

While the Draft stated that UNFPA could go beyond the United Nations system in choosing an organization to provide technical assistance, it also made it clear that the Fund did not regard itself as an executing agency in the usual sense of the term. That is, it did not propose to build up its own staff to the point where it would be in direct competition with the Agencies in providing technical assistance within the terms of their respective mandates. It would have been a rash act to do so. In one stroke the Fund would have lost the experience, competence, and support of the organizations in the United Nations system and perhaps, in some cases, governmental approval as well.

The Draft also provided that "in administering the Fund, the Administrator may also call on the assistance of other UNDP staff, and, where appropriate, the Fund will reimburse UNDP for these services". The reasoning here was that UNDP financial support services and personnel administration were going concerns and that it would be advantageous for the Fund to utilize them. It would also contribute to keeping down overhead costs. Regarding the allocation of UNFPA resources for programme and administration, both Hoffman and later Petersen, when he took over as Administrator, left the policy decisions to the Executive Director. These various managerial arrangements gave the Fund the financial autonomy and flexibility it needed.

The Draft said that "the terms of reference of the Fund encompass assistance on all aspects of population which have an important bearing on economic and social development, and education, research and data gathering or any relevant factors may be supported. No population policy, and indeed no serious economic and social plans, can be formulated unless they are based on sound demographic and statistical foundations."

As I have already mentioned, the United Nations Secretariat had already made very important contributions in analysis, projections, and technical assistance in the demographic field, and I was convinced that much of the Fund's resources must go to continuing and increasing this work. There were still many countries which only had the vaguest notion of their demographic situation and had little concept of the need for population data in their economic and social planning.

In addition, I reasoned that since we were aiming at universal participation, there would be a large number of governments which would see and approve the utility of initiating programmes on statistics and demography but which would oppose or be reluctant to launch into family planning projects, at least until they had sufficient knowledge of their population situations. It is interesting to note that within a few years the Fund was helping fifteen African countries to conduct censuses for the first time in their history. Some of these countries have now taken a further step forward and recognize the value of family planning for the health and well-being of their citizens.

Expanding the Fund's terms of reference to cover "all aspects of population" was quite a different matter. The Fund was now going deliberately beyond the bounds of the safe precincts of population statistics and demography, which, after all, stop when the situation has been charted, and was preparing to move in on population pressure areas and help do something about them.

On this point the Fund deliberately stated its intention of assisting countries with action programmes including family planning in the field of population. In retrospect this seemed an obvious move but, at that time, little assistance had been given to countries with family planning programmes. Moreover, no United Nations organization had a legislative mandate that permitted it to supply contraceptives. I reasoned, however, that a population fund which could not help requesting countries with family planning would be no population fund at all. Furthermore, a fund which did help countries to do what they wanted to do would be respected even by countries not themselves in favour of government-sponsored family planning programmes.

Virtually every government I spoke to was, happily, of this opinion. Anxious to move in this direction, we decided, as our first major project, to respond to an urgent request from the Egyptian Government to finance a large supply of contraceptives for its family planning programme.

The Draft also cautiously, but deliberately, opened the door in another direction by undertaking to provide assistance with local and recurrent

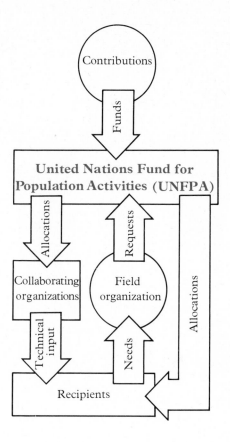

FIG. 1. How the UNFPA operates.

costs not ordinarily borne by United Nations organizations. We recognized of course, that to succeed a project had to enjoy priority with the governments, and that perhaps the best test of this was the extent to which governments were willing to put up their own funds, facilities, or personnel. We thought, however, it necessary in order to be effective to be more generous in population programmes than in other types of economic and social programmes.

Although political leaders and planners may be convinced of the need for moderation of population growth rates, when it comes to the agonizing business of allocating scarce resources among competitive demands, programmes which promise short-term benefits are likely to get preference over the usually longer-term population undertakings. A judicious use of external funds in local cost financing might increase the priority given to population programmes of longer duration.

The general operations model for the work UNFPA envisioned in the Draft is shown in Fig. 1.

Fundraising: First Stage

The next point on my mental inventory of first steps to be taken was the need for increased funds. Here we got much help from Hoffman, himself a formidable fundraiser, and from his friend William H. Draper, another first-rate money-extractor. Draper, an irrepressible gentleman already in the second half of his seventies, was a prominent figure on the American scene. He had already had several highly successful careers as businessman, soldier, and government administrator. He had played a key role in America's assistance to Germany and Japan after World War II and had won the lasting respect and gratitude of their leaders in the process. Latterly he committed himself to be fundraiser *extraordinaire* for population causes and had had a hand in getting increased United States Congressional support for population programmes and in raising money to expand the work of IPPF. Among his various activities were to serve on the board of IPPF, to act as Honorary Chairman of the Population Crisis Committee, and to represent the United States on the United Nations Population Commission. One of Hoffman's first acts on getting the Secretary-General's letter asking him to administer UNFPA was to ask

Draper to become his consultant on fundraising.

At the start our fundraiser was Hoffman himself. Early in my acquaintance with him I had wondered how he had made such great strides in his career: in Studebaker, the Marshall Plan, the Ford Foundation, the United Nations. Then one day I was in his office, and a problem came up involving delicate relationships among his officers. Suddenly I became aware that his face had lit up and his eyes sparkled as I had never seen them. It came to me that this was where his talent really lay. He had a fantastic knowledge of people, a great ability to communicate with them, and a tremendous sincerity of purpose.

To return to late 1969. I was beginning to learn the ropes. One thing was immediately apparent—fundraising efforts never cease. My own initial attempt was to visit Maurice Strong who was then the head of the Canadian International Development Agency. It was my first experience of soliciting funds. What would have happened if Strong had not given me a warm welcome followed a month later by a handsome check I cannot imagine. But he sent me on my way feeling that I had found a new and interesting profession as a salesman. I have been on the road ever since.

Practically every approach we could think of was made to governments both from developed and developing countries. Draper believed in persistence. In Japan, former Prime Minister Nobusuke Kishi whom he knew intimately, affectionately called him the "Draper Typhoon". He says this even today in full appreciation of his dynamism and with esteem for the man to whom he could not resist giving money. Draper also initiated "See for Yourself" trips for the parliamentarians of two of our largest donor countries. These were trips to congested population areas in Asia to see at first hand what population pressure meant and what countries were doing about it. These trips were so successful that the parliamentarians upon return to their home countries recommended that the contributions to UNFPA be doubled. And we got them in the next round of pledges.

Parallel to Draper's persistent efforts I made the same points in lower key, particularly with the leaders of the developing countries. I believed that if governments would only take a closer look at their own population situations as well as those of others there would be no doubt of their willingness to undertake population activities and to help with the money needed to support them. Whatever the magic formula—persistence, reasoning, or maybe the good intent of governments was perhaps already there and only in need of a little nudging—the Fund's initial financial difficulties soon vanished.

Hoffman, Draper, and I agreed that the 1970 fundraising target for UNFPA would be $15 million, of which it was hoped the United States would supply half on a matching basis. Most of the balance we decided to seek from other governments of industrialized countries. Contributions of a million dollars or more were indeed received for 1970 from Canada, the Federal Republic of Germany, Japan, Sweden, and the United Kingdom, which together with other important contributions from Denmark, Finland, Netherlands, and Norway were matched by the United States.

Despite our strategy of getting most of our money from the industrialized world, we had also agreed it would be very important to get as many developing countries as possible to participate in the Fund as donors as well as recipients. This was a matter for which I considered myself particularly responsible. I was very gratified when in 1970 Cyprus, the Dominican Republic, India, Indonesia, Iran, Mauritius, Pakistan, the Philippines, Sri Lanka, Somalia, Trinidad and Tobago, and Tunisia started to contribute to the Fund. For the first time I felt that we were off to a flying start with support from all areas of the world.

Establishment of Advisory Groups

As a Trust Fund of the Secretary-General, UNFPA had no intergovernmental board directing its operations but took its authority solely from the Secretary-General acting within a general mandate from the General Assembly and the Economic and Social Council. On thinking things over, however, U Thant, Hoffman, and I decided that it would be important for the Fund to explain its policies and operations to influential people in various regions of the world for the dual purpose of obtaining their advice and guidance and of enlisting their aid in making the Fund better known in their countries. Accordingly, we agreed that a number of prominent and distinguished persons should be invited to serve in their private capacities on an Advisory Board. The nature of the Board and the identity of the participants were matters on which the Secretary-General, Hoffman, C. V. Narasimhan, and I spent much time.

A quite outstanding panel was the result. Dr. Alberto Lleras-Camargo, the former President of Colombia, was designated Chairman. Among the others were Lord Caradon, the former Permanent Representative of the United Kingdom to the United Nations; Erhard Eppler, Minister for Economic Cooperation of the Federal Republic of Germany; Leo Mates, Director of the Institute of International Politics and Economy in Yugoslavia; Tage Erlander, former Prime Minister of Sweden; Maurice Strong; and John D. Rockefeller 3rd, from industrialized countries. Aziz Ahmed, then Foreign Secretary and now Foreign Minister of Pakistan; Angie Brooks, Assistant Secretary of State of Liberia and former President of the United Nations General Assembly; and Roesia Sardjono, Secretary-General of Social Development of the Department of Social Affairs of Indonesia, were among representatives from developing countries. All the Executive Secretaries of the United Nations regional economic commissions also were members.

The life of this Committee was shortened when the rapid growth of the Fund led the General Assembly in 1972 to give the Fund a formal intergovernmental board. But from it the Fund derived many of its initial contacts and understandings with countries all over the world. We owe thanks to all its members for their sound and practical counsel and their help at a critical period in the Fund's development.

Consultations with the United Nations Organizations

We also recognized that we would need close relations with the organizations of the United Nations system with capabilities in the population field, most of which would execute the projects funded by UNFPA. They were the United Nations Department of Economic and Social Affairs, including the regional economic commissions, UNICEF, UNIDO (United Nations Industrial Development Organization), UNDP, ILO, FAO, UNESCO, WHO, the World Bank, and the World Food Programme. It was, indeed, suggested at one time that UNFPA should have representatives of at least some of those organizations on its staff. I did not want, however, to have our own staff work done by people who, however constructive and capable they might be, would be primarily under the supervision and direction of another organization. Thus it was agreed that we would meet twice a year with the representatives of these organizations as a UNFPA Inter-Agency Consultative Committee under our chairmanship. We had many operational problems to discuss with them. In addition, while we made it clear that responsibility for UNFPA's action was its alone, I wanted us always to discuss important matters of policy with the executing agencies and take their points of view into account.

One time early in my stay in New York, an Ambassador asked me: "How do you, at Director level, expect to coordinate the United Nations Agencies, which go their own way anyway?" I replied that I never said that I would coordinate them: "I will get them to coordinate me." To this end, in 1969 I called on the Directors-General of ILO, FAO, UNESCO, and WHO to pay my respects and to enlist their support for the Fund's programme. I was pleasantly surprised by their open attitude towards the idea of expanding the population work of their agencies. Of special interest to me was the WHO because of the close relationship of its mandate to family planning.

At that time Dr. M. G. Candau from Brazil was the Director-General. He had done much to build that Agency into the really strong and influential organization that it is. He was reputed not to spend more than half an hour with anyone with my kind of business. But when I called on him at his Geneva headquarters he gave me half the day, provided me with an interesting insight into his management practices, showed me WHO's beautiful new building and rose gardens, and invited me for lunch. It was quite obvious that he was personally most interested in the Fund's capacity to help in expanding WHO's clinical work to give greater emphasis to family planning and to related medical training, though as a result of earlier heated debates in his own governing body he was still proceeding with some caution. In fact, the World Health Assembly had only recently reached agreement on its mandate on family planning, human reproduction, and population dynamics based on the concept of family health.

It is interesting to note that almost coincidentally with the advent of UNFPA, the organization set up a Family Health Division and planned a rather comprehensive programme on the medical and health aspects of family planning and population dynamics—a programme that was subsequently given considerable impetus by steady injections of supplementary funds from UNFPA. Incidentally one of the main negotiators of Fund support for this programme was Halfdan Mahler who later succeeded Candau as Director-General of the Organization.

Candau, I should like to add, went on record a little later saying: "The mandate of WHO while recognizing that the question of family size remains a matter for the free and exclusive choice of the individual family affirms that every family should have the opportunity to obtain information and advice on problems of family planning."

In my initial visits to ILO I found the officials of this organization very receptive to the idea of opening up new undertakings in population, particularly as ILO was passing through a period of acute financial stringency and the prospect of funded projects in population was especially attractive. Having spoken with David Morse, the then Director-General of ILO, and his number two man who later succeeded him, Wilfred Jenks, I had no doubts that UNFPA would have the whole-hearted cooperation of this organization. The ILO position was clarified by Jenks when he said: "No lasting solution of the employment problem can be envisaged without moderating the excessive high rates of population growth now prevalent." As a consequence the ILO action programmes in the last few years, under the guidance of the present Director-General Francis Blanchard, have always given due consideration to the population factor.

Like ILO, FAO was only too eager to discuss possible field programmes—in this case affecting rural communities. A. H. Boerma, who succeeded B. R. Sen, had taken up the crusade where his predecessor had left off and become one of the most outspoken commentators on the population situation in relation to world food supplies.

Realizing that it would be by no means easy to respond to country requests and to instigate programmes which would fall within the mandates of the Agencies executing the programmes, we sought to get the Agencies to appoint at a senior level a coordinator of their population work with whom we could deal and who could deal with us. All did so promptly with the exception of UNESCO, which delayed making a similar appointment to meet the reservations of René Maheu, its former Director-General, who was at first reluctant to expand UNESCO's role in population.

I was somewhat concerned about the degree to which UNFPA involuntarily was already committed to building up the staffs of these organizations. Both Hoffman and I considered that the purpose of the Fund was to help countries and that any other activities that it engaged in would have to be justified in these terms—in fact and not just semantically. As I have already mentioned, I was thus not happy to have it prescribed that United Nations administrative costs, "infrastructure" is the United Nations bureaucratize for it, would be a first charge against the Fund.

I recognized, however, that the capabilities of the system would have to be built up before it would be in a position to be of much help to countries. It was clear that until a large volume of programming had developed, the UNDP method of covering Agency central expenses through paying overhead as a set percentage of programming costs would be inflexible and restrictive. There would also be advantages to having some personnel in the Agencies who had a direct interest in seeing that they discharged the Fund's business in satisfactory fashion.

The Programme Consultative Committee

The third major group with which we had to have close relations consisted of organizations outside the United Nations system which had parallel programmes. Obviously, for both technical and economic reasons, we had to coordinate our programmes with theirs. Accordingly, we set up a Programme Consultative Committee (PCC), which also met twice a year.

We invited representatives of the international development agencies, or other appropriate organizations, of Canada, Denmark, the Federal Republic of Germany, Finland, Japan, Netherlands, Norway, Sweden, the United Kingdom, and the United States to take part, as well as representatives of the Ford Foundation, the Population Council, the Rockefeller Foundation, the International Planned Parenthood Federation, the World Bank, and the Organization for Economic Cooperation and Development (OECD) to serve on it. Subsequently several other governments were invited to attend.

The PCC, like the Advisory Board, gave way later to the formal governing body, but was of crucial importance in this early phase in that our principal donors were represented and, what was equally important, were represented by their principal population officers. These were at one and the same time the people whose support we needed the most and from whose estrangement we would have had the most to fear.

Participating at the formative stage in discussion of the Fund's policies, plans, and programmes they felt they knew what we were up to. At the same time we were in a position to profit from their experience with programmes similar to our own. It was also vital that the principal population officers of the foundations understood us. They too had great influence and great experience. I doubt that the Fund would have survived its first years without the successful functioning of this body, strange hybrid that it was.

Government Forums

I also did my best to introduce the Fund to important international bodies concerned with population and development. The first of these was certainly the United Nations Population Commission. This Commission is an intergovernmental body under ECOSOC which meets at least once every two years to guide the work of the United Nations Secretariat in population. The member countries are usually represented by their leading demographers or senior government officials concerned with population.

As it was important that the Commission should be fully informed, I addressed its 15th Session in 1969 in Geneva to make that body aware of recent developments and plans concerning the Fund. I made it clear that programmes executed by the Specialized Agencies and UNICEF were now eligible for financing, that the Fund's scope had been broadened to cover types of aid other than the usual forms of technical assistance, and that it could now provide equipment and supplies and support local programme costs. I emphasized that the Secretary-General and the Administrator intended the Fund to be "action oriented", that is, to concentrate on country programmes.

I also indicated the important role the Fund might play in coordinating United Nations system efforts: "Since population problems relate to the total fabric of a society, projects and programmes will, in many cases, not break down neatly along the lines of academic disciplines or organizational jurisdictions. An imaginative approach and the closest possible cooperation and coordination of population projects and programmes will be required among the various elements of the United Nations system." I made much the same points a few days later in an address to the Development Centre of the Organization for Economic Cooperation and Development (OECD) in Paris.

I had been anxious to establish contact with OECD with its influential membership representative of the main European countries, North America, and Japan. Designed to promote economic growth and stability in its member countries and consequently to make a contribution to the expansion of the world economy, the Organization had good relationships with developing countries particularly through the activities of its Development Assistance Committee (DAC). Philander Claxton, the Special Assistant on Population to the US Secretary of State, was presiding officer at the meeting I attended. As Claxton had been closely associated with the Fund since its early years and, indeed, had a lot to do with its formulation and policies, I could not have had a better introduction from the chair nor a more receptive audience.

These were valuable opportunities to introduce the Fund to some of the most important people in the population and development fields in donor and recipient governments. In them I had my first chance to emphasize the Fund's desire to be responsive to the wishes of countries and to be flexible so that it could adapt its procedures to the different situations in different countries. Emphasis on the "action orientation" of the Fund was, of course, a promise that the Fund would move as quickly as possible towards an intensive field programme directed towards ensuring that appropriate assistance was delivered promptly to the recipient.

These wide initial consultations set a pattern for succeeding years. As one staff member remarked, not entirely cynically, never before have so few consulted with so many. Looking back, I am appalled to think of the number of hours, airplane miles, cups of coffee in the Delegates Lounge, and luncheons, and dinners here and around the world that I devoted to establishing communications. Enough to win most elective offices, which in a way was what UNFPA had to do.

CHAPTER 4

The Promotional Phase

The rate of growth of our programme, of course, was determined in the first instance by the rate of growth of our contributions. In opting for an attempt to secure a very rapid rise in our contributions in order to launch a very visible programme right from the start, we were taking an important policy decision. It could have been argued, and was by some, that a cautious, step-by-step approach to programming would be best with good results secured on a small scale before the programme was expanded. For several reasons, however, I could not accept this line of reasoning.

From the beginning, we concentrated a formidable amount of time, thought, and energy on encouraging developing countries to tackle their population situations with the promise of international assistance in doing so, on stimulating enthusiastic interest and financial support among donor nations, and on enlisting the cooperation of organizations best equipped to assist in carrying out population operations.

Countries considering the pros and cons of embarking on population work needed reassurance that the Fund's assistance would be sufficiently substantial to be worth bothering about—for dealing with any external source of assistance is, indeed, a bother—before they would be inclined to move at all. Donor countries had to be shown urgency matched with action if they were to make, and increase, their contributions. And the organizations helping to implement the projects had to be persuaded that population programmes represented an expansion of their own work and not merely a set of new problems and strains.

The only way to accomplish this, as I saw it, was to assemble a critical mass of resources and to programme them as quickly as possible. I have never regretted this course. If UNFPA had been willing to remain an insignificant factor for the first two years I am convinced that it would still be an insignificant factor.

Lest I give the impression that too much emphasis was laid on money matters, let me explain that fundraising is the major bogey haunting anyone engaged in promoting humanitarian undertakings. I have listened to many impassioned speeches on the infamy of putting dollar, sterling, or other currency tags on programmes which stem from some nobility in the spirit of man. But in this pragmatic world I have noticed that the spirit is all the better for some solid financial backing.

Apparently our efforts had some kind of catalytic effect on both potential donors and recipients, for a flow of contributions came just in time to meet an unexpectedly high wave of requests. Overnight, it seemed to me, my original twelve projects became five hundred, and we had to shift gears swiftly and move towards a greatly accelerated programming process.

The rise in project requests, at this early point, emanated mainly from the Department of Economic and Social Affairs and other United Nations organizations. The upsurge of direct requests from governments came later. Consequently, much of the Fund's assistance from the end of 1969 over the subsequent two years was absorbed by activities which would strengthen the capabilities of the system to provide technical assistance in the population field.

The United Nations was now moving into an area in which, with the exception of technical assistance in population statistics and demographic training and research, it had been doing little or nothing. It was thus not unreasonable that, at the outset, the bulk of the Fund's allocations were made for interregional or regional projects implemented by the United Nations, its regional economic commissions, and other organizations. Most of these were designed to demonstrate what the United Nations system could offer and to draw the attention of potential recipients to the possibilities of population aid.

What we had in mind was a promotional phase. Over the longer run we meant to give priority to requests for country programmes.

As it turned out, we were able to handle more country requests than anticipated and also build up the capabilities of the United Nations system. Some idea of the degree of acceleration is given by the following figures. By the end of 1969, a total of less than $3 million had been committed to projects by the Fund. By 31 December 1972 the Fund had made allocations of over $50 million for 470 country, regional, and interregional projects covering all aspects of population.

The Agencies' viewpoint on Fund programming was clear and predictable. They wished to see more regional and interregional undertakings or well-tailored population appendages to projects in their respective specialized spheres. Their arguments were sound insofar as they went.

The WHO attitude, which was explained at a number of meetings by Albert Zahra, laid emphasis on that Organization's unquestioned expertise in health areas. The policy line adhered to was that the WHO should, with the help of UNFPA, take the leadership role in the world on the medical and health aspects of family planning and population dynamics. This, it was maintained, would make it possible for governments who were not ready to initiate national population programmes to take the less controversial route of integrating family planning with existing health programmes.

WHO also indicated it wished to be an active partner in all undertakings concerned with epidemiological research, particularly in such critical areas as human reproduction, women and child bearing, abortion and contraceptives, and in setting up multidisciplinary training centres which might be brought into operation in cooperation with other agencies such as UNICEF, UNESCO and ILO. The Fund did help WHO to expand its various activities on epidemiological and health demography subjects at interregional and regional levels as well as to undertake greatly increased country activities in the health and population field without, however, relinquishing the Fund's right to supervisory control over projects receiving its support.

WHO has always worked closely with UNICEF which, under the very effective direction of Henry Labouisse and his Deputy Charles Egger, has an excellent record in activities associated with the welfare of mothers and children. At a very early date UNICEF became the primary supplier of contraceptives for UNFPA-supported family planning programmes. Later this Organization developed a stockpile for contraceptives and family planning equipment with the help of a bloc allocation from UNFPA. This cut costs and improved coordination and speed of deliveries.

ILO approaches to the Fund were primarily concerned with the influence of population trends on employment. Kailas Doctor, the ILO's representative, strongly advocated the introduction of population components to ongoing development projects being funded by other organizations including UNDP. Reasonably enough, ILO proposed a series of projects concerned with improving the population education of industrial workers which involved influential cadres such as trade union secretariats and labour leaders. ILO also started an exploration of vocational training and cooperative rural development programmes to see how they could be adjusted to take in the new element.

A similar view on adjustment of existing programmes was advanced by W. Schulte on behalf of FAO, to the effect that his Organization could diffuse population information in its rural education and agricultural extension schemes and highlight relationships between population, food consumption, and agricultural productivity to assist in agricultural planning and policy formulation. Profiting from programmes already in operation, of course, had always been a UNFPA approach.

Finally, UNESCO saw regional structures as the prerequisites for successful national projects in the communications and education field in that they ensured more effective recruitment of experts, speedier delivery of national programmes in the region and stimulated cross-fertilization of ideas. Consequently the projects proposed by this Agency through Alexander Graham sought financing for interregional and regional projects in population education and communications methodology.

Along with the work of the United Nations Population Division the Regional Economic Commissions played their part well. After I had made initial contacts with the Executive Secretaries of the various Economic Commissions—U Nyun and Johan Maramis in ESCAP, Robert Gardiner in ECA, Carlos Quintana and Enrique Iglesias in ECLA, Mohamed Said Al-Attar in ECWA, and J. Stanovnik in ECE—the Fund was able to stimulate a substantial increase in the population activities of all these Commissions. These included sponsoring or otherwise supporting regional training programmes on population censuses and data collection, carrying out fertility and migration studies, and keeping national population policies continuously under review.

The work of all these United Nations organizations in developing regional and interregional projects not only greatly advanced knowledge about population matters but also helped and encouraged governments with their national undertakings. These projects were carried out in addition to technical assistance services provided to UNFPA-funded country projects.

This brief résumé barely does justice to the scope of the contribution of these interregional and regional activities. I should like to emphasize, however, that the test of their usefulness was the degree of their usefulness to national efforts. I think it has been well demonstrated that projects of this kind are an essential link between national and international efforts. They give countries training advantages they could not individually afford. They provide services in areas of common concern, such as research, which would be too complex and costly for countries to undertake by themselves. The results of the training and research programmes of the regional institutes add immeasurably to our general stock of knowledge as to how population programmes can be formulated and conducted.

In contrast with the well-defined positions and approaches of the Agencies and the Regional Economic Commissions, the requests emanating directly from governments were in the beginning sporadic, usually reflecting an immediate need, and, except in the case of countries where population programmes had already started, were often very imprecise. This was to be expected. For many officials it was their first confrontation with population factors and their effects on national, social, and economic development. It also represented their first steps towards introducing policies and strategies which might be opposed by certain sections of their populace.

We did not mind funding a wide range of relatively diversified small projects. By doing so we hoped to further our objective of universal participation and at the same time fulfil our stated commitment to provide countries with the kind of help they asked in the form in which they wished it. We also laid the foundation for what in many instances became large well-rounded national programmes in countries such as Bangladesh, Bolivia, Costa Rica, the Dominican Republic, Ecuador, Jamaica, and Kenya.

I admit that it would have been considerably easier for the Fund to accede to Agency wishes and to build up a programme of population assistance along the lines they suggested, thus virtually making them the arbitrators of the national programming. But the Fund's primary responsibility was to help countries to identify and clarify their population situations and then to assist them in tackling the problems in whatever form they arose. Therefore, even at the expense of accepting some government requests that did not fit too well with our concepts of long-term strategies which would make real impact, we did so confident that the governments themselves by the very act of involvement would move eventually towards population activities more effectively integrated with their overall development plans—and indeed this is what happened.

Melding the proposed programmes of the United Nations system with that of the individual governments was a process that could have benefited from the wisdom of Solomon. But somehow or other compromises were made and positions modified so that it proved possible to start moving on a series of field activities which brought United Nations expertise, competence, and experience to bear on population matters without stifling the initiative, thrust, and good intent of the governments or without infringing on their dominions. Above all, the Fund was able to keep a measure of control over events and to improve its position as central coordinator of worldwide population activities.

While in some respects the programme in the first few years appeared to be somewhat diffuse, it was truly astonishing how quickly it sharpened up and became stamped with national characteristics. This was particularly noticeable in the regional patterns.

In South and South-East Asia, for example, where population density was great and living standards relatively low, most governments had already identified their population problems and had introduced measures aimed at encouraging reductions in fertility for both economic and social reasons. Consequently when help from the Fund became available, they were first in line to ask for assistance in improving delivery systems and other elements in their family planning programmes, thus making family planning the dominant feature of population work in that region.

In Africa, however, lack of basic demographic data and the machinery and skills required for the collection, analysis, and use of such information led countries, with the advice and guidance of the Regional Economic Commission for Africa, to approach the Fund for help in building up such services and in conducting censuses, often in an initial move towards national modernization.

In Latin America where growth rates were high and urbanization a major problem the programmes were a mixture of analytical work and family planning. Studies of the link between social sciences and population had been given considerable impetus by the Chile-based demographic institute CELADE and by the Regional Economic Commission for Latin America. CELADE, which was originally assisted by the UNDP and later by UNFPA, had been a source of technical and advisory services to the countries of the region for many years. The governments were therefore in a position to assess quickly their population imbalances and to take appropriate action towards the inclusion of family planning in national health programmes. By the time the Fund came along requests began to even up between demographic projects and family planning.

The Next Programming Stage

While the regional patterns were emerging from a mix of Agency programmes, some fairly sound governmental requests and others of less significance, several Asian countries which were fully aware of their population dilemmas, moved into a new stage. Disappointed by existing family planning programmes which had fallen short of expectations and were absorbing heavy financial inputs, they began considering the possibility of launching large-scale population undertakings which would cover all aspects and be closely interrelated to other development programmes.

This is precisely what the Fund hoped would happen as countries advanced from the concept of individual projects towards the formulation of an overall population strategy. From any point of view—that of the Government, the Agencies, and the Fund—it was a new and exciting prospect both for action and international cooperation.

The Fund's first country agreement for a comprehensive population programme was worked out with the Government of Pakistan. On 27 August 1970 an agreement was signed in Islamabad which called for over $1.7 million in assistance from us over the first twelve months of a five-year programme, further financing to be provided later on. It was an ambitious project, directed towards improving motivational techniques and providing support for a wide range of family planning programmes including salary supplements for field workers, contraceptive supplies, and land and river transport. Central facilities were to be expanded through the establishment of two training, research, and evaluation centres, and the strengthening of maternal and child health services including a *post-partum* programme in selected hospitals.

Moreover, the Pakistan government stipulated that UNFPA should station a "Senior Adviser" in Islamabad as an assistant to the UNDP Resident Representative to help him in taking care of UNFPA's obligations under the Agreement. This was the opening wedge for the subsequent campaign to get the field staff unified and more firmly under our control.

As can be imagined, such an agreement was not arrived at overnight. The whole venture had its beginning in a joint United Nations/WHO mission which in 1968, at the request of the government, had studied Pakistan's national family planning programme and had made recommendations for improvement and expansion, including the addition of other population components. Before long these recommendations reappeared in the form of requests for assistance from the Fund.

At Fund headquarters we had long and involved discussions on how to proceed. Whatever we did we would be breaking new ground and establishing precedents of some consequence. A comprehensive programme would inevitably demand expertise from a number of sources. One primary concern, therefore, was to devise a formula which would define the duties and responsibilities of all parties—the Government, the Agencies, and the Fund. A mechanism was also required which would permit the implementation of the various components of the programme in a logical manner as part of an interrelated network.

The Pakistan agreement, although it had its shortcomings, did have all the features of what quickly became an important UNFPA-programming strategy.

Firstly, since it covered a number of years, it provided a long-term perspective of the volume and kinds of assistance to be furnished by the Fund. Secondly, it gave an overall framework for future programming and established the structure and points of authority in both the government and the United Nations system and coordinating committees. Thus it did much to help draw together the various elements of our assistance to the country into a planned whole made up of mutually supporting elements. Thirdly, the assistance was programmed in accordance with the priority needs identified by the government. Fourthly, the effective cooperation and participation of the Executing Agencies of the United Nations system and other non-governmental organizations was sought at the earliest programming stage and, finally, by channelling the assistance from these organizations through one central unit, the government was able to coordinate all external assistance in the population field.

It would be less than truthful to say that from then on we lived happily ever after. Country programming taught us and continues to teach us some hard lessons. A case in point was the negotiation of the second country agreement—that with Mauritius. There had been several missions to Mauritius by one or another part of the United Nations system: one from WHO, one from UNDP, and one from the International Bank for Reconstruction and Development (World Bank). In the latter case a detailed, and on the face of it well-thought-out programme had been drawn up by a highly qualified foreign expert. It called for the Government to take over from private organizations the provision of family planning services by a division of Maternal and Child Health and Family Planning in the Ministry of Health. After developing this programme the World Bank, for reasons of its own, decided not to fund it and the Government asked us to step in.

Because of the length of time the negotiations were taking with one or another part of the United Nations system, we felt under pressure to be brisk. By cable we stated our interest in funding the programme and fielded an inter-agency mission to negotiate an agreement. When the mission got to Mauritius its members agreed that it would be a wise move for the Government to assume the responsibility for providing family planning services on a phased basis, a district or two at a time, so that difficulties encountered in the first could be taken into account in the second. In the meantime, the Mauritian Cabinet had approved the Bank expert's plan which had thus become government policy, and there was no mention of phased implementation.

The UNFPA-led team then agreed to do what we really, in our haste, had committed ourselves to do, that is, help the Government to carry out the expert's plan. It turned out as our mission had feared. For reasons of pay scales, civil service regulations, etc., the incorporation of personnel of the Mauritius Family Planning Association into the Ministry of Health, called for in the plan, involved all sorts of difficulties and caused seemingly interminable delays. The lesson was clear. By all means send a negotiating or programming mission when it is called for. But in agreeing with a government to do so, be sure of what is being agreed to in the process.

The Fund's third country agreement came in April 1971, greatly broadening our assistance to Egypt. A sum of $1,250,000 was programmed for the first year of the agreement and the Fund guaranteed support for the balance of a five-year period at a level warranted by operations. Included in the first year were such projects as a pilot maternity-centred programme, a biomedical research programme, the introduction of family planning education in schools, workers' training schemes, and in other adult and youth programmes, and the provision of contraceptive supplies.

It was, I think, very opportune that in the early stages of international population assistance UNFPA was asked for help by Pakistan and Egypt. They were, at that time, among the relatively few Muslim countries conscious of the impact of demographic pressures on their economic and social development.

UNFPA sought to broaden its approach to the 600 million-member Muslim world in December 1971 through support for a conference held by the IPPF in Rabat, Morocco, to discuss "Islam and Planned Parenthood". Some eighty distinguished theologians and secular Muslim scholars from throughout the world gathered in their personal capacities to consider the relationship between social development and demographic trends. At that conference UNFPA mentioned the possibility of supporting a population studies centre in Al Azhar University in Cairo, the oldest and most respected university in the Muslim world. This institution has a student body of some 38,000, of which some 22 per cent are from Muslim countries other than Egypt.

We thought that a population studies centre there would be particularly effective in catering to the needs of Muslims throughout the world. Scholars had indicated a wish to study why Muslim communities and minorities within other populations often had common features of low productivity, low personal income, low literacy, and high fertility. A programme for the centre in Al Azhar University was drawn up very carefully by the faculty of the University in consultation with members of a group, led by Sir Colville Deverell, former head of the IPPF. A proposal for a first phase of this project to be assisted by UNFPA was finally approved by the Governing Council at its June 1975 Session.

By the end of 1972 we had concluded five other comprehensive agreements: Iran on 9 November 1971 after a successful mission headed by Lord Caradon; Thailand on 12 November 1971; the Philippines on 14 January 1972; Indonesia on 18 April 1972; and Chile on 9 June 1972.

The Chile agreement was still another landmark in the Fund's progress in that Chile was the first country on the South American continent to launch a government-sponsored programme with family planning components. The Government had exclusively social—not demographic—goals in providing family planning services and they were presented within a maternal and child health programme. But it was a major programme and also it was being undertaken by a socialist administration. I signed the agreement in the presence of the late President of Chile, Salvador Allende Gossens.

Even though President Allende and his Government had every intention of conducting a serious family-planning programme within the context of maternal and child health, sensitivities were such that on my arrival in Santiago they asked me never to mention the words "family planning" or "birth control". When the President spoke at the signing ceremony he referred only to the health services as the area in which United Nations assistance was being furnished. Since we in the Fund were in no way dogmatic, this presented no problems for me. We were interested in realities, not semantics, and recognized that all sorts of people have all sorts of problems which deserve respect.

The Indonesian agreement is also worthy of note because it was a joint project between the Fund and the World Bank. The reasons for and consequences of this require a little background.

In UNFPA, as I have already emphasized, we were anxious to cooperate with the United Nations Secretariat, its Regional Economic Commissions, and the Specialized Agencies. At the same time we did not want the Agencies to stand between us and the recipient countries. Consequently we were careful that the programmes we approved were those the recipient countries really wanted and not those that the Agencies might conceive to be proper for them. In this regard the Fund from time to time emerged as the catalyser of somewhat divergent views.

We had already decided to experiment with executing some projects through IPPF. Eventually quite an important project was executed this way in Mexico. For several reasons, however, use of the IPPF as an executing agency in Indonesia was not appropriate. Our eye then lit on the World Bank, which was developing a population programme of its own. A member of the United Nations system, it is a somewhat separate one, having quite a different pattern of funding, programming, and implementation from the rest. Both we and the Bank had been talking to Indonesia, and UNFPA had a substantial programming start there already. Why not put together a single package, fund it jointly, and let the Bank have the key role in the execution of the programme. This would extend our scope and at the same time demonstrate further that there were other channels through which we could operate in addition to those offered by the Agencies.

The programme we eventually worked out called for $13.2 million each from UNFPA and the Bank plus another $6.4 million from the Government over a five-year period. This was by far our largest country programme up to that time and proved to be too complex for the experiment. The differences between the regular United Nations system approach and the methods used by the Bank were so many and the Agencies' concern at their reduced role was so great that we soon found ourselves enmeshed in endless difficulties. The patience of all concerned was sorely tried before the programme got smoothly under way. Nevertheless, the problems we had in this case showed us what was needed for better coordination in UNFPA and World Bank population programming.

I found several conversations with Robert MacNamara, President of the World Bank, at Bellagio and in Washington most instructive. Not only was he a major force in putting population problems on the world agenda but his analytic grasp of the situation gave me the cues where the emphasis of our programmes should be. Through his understanding of our work and the cooperation of his Director of Population and Nutrition Projects, Dr. K. Kanagaratnam, excellent working relations have been built between the Fund and the Bank.

Another relationship tangle developed in connection with proposals for a multidisciplinary International Population Institute for training and research. We had agreed to do a feasibility study. This was conducted by a high-powered group led by David Morse, the former Director-General of ILO. It renamed the putative institution the World Population Institute and proposed to give it a great strength and formidable powers. This again worried the United Nations organizations which had always wished to take a dominant part in the substantive aspects of programming. It was also interpreted by some of our donors as a renewed attempt by the Department of Economic and Social Affairs to make the decisions on the uses of UNFPA resources. As a result of opposition from these quarters and a less than convincing defence by its proponents, the proposal lost the support of the members of the Population Commission in November 1971. The Fund has subsequently helped to develop a less imposing regionalized training programme.

Such organizational concerns may sound petty. But if one is to run a large-scale action programme, questions of authority and control are of consequence. But these were special cases and for every "difficult" case we had a hundred projects in which all the organizations concerned were working effectively together.

Making the Fund Known

In spite of all this activity in the early days even recipients of Fund support were hardly conscious of its existence. They were receiving help through one or another of the United Nations organizations and often did not distinguish between projects we were funding and other activities of that agency. As late as December 1971, at the first demographic conference in Africa, which the Fund had fully financed, when I was introduced to one of the participants as the head of UNFPA, he responded "What's that?" If the Fund was to be built up, have status in the eyes of governments, and be universally recognized as the operational arm of the United Nations for population, it had to have a clear identity.

Initially, the courting of awareness was done by maintaining close contacts with the Permanent Missions to the United Nations of donor and recipient countries in New York and during travels by myself and members of the staff. Later, as our system of programme delivery became better established, the Resident Representatives and our Coordinators came to represent a very live UNFPA presence in the recipient countries.

The Fund has always kept the Permanent Missions fully informed on programmes and operations. This has paid handsome dividends in discussions in United Nations forums. I have spent a great deal of time talking to Chiefs of Mission, Counsellors, and Mission officers down to the rank of Second Secretary, and am sure I have been one of the few Under Secretaries-General to talk regularly to the latter.

I have always been very encouraged by the interest expressed by various ambassadors, many of whom have become intimately acquainted with the Fund's operations and problems. Since I also sought to have close contacts with other Mission officers I instituted the practice of holding group briefings. Some of the officers, particularly those in small Missions from developing countries, were responsible for a very wide range of United Nations activities and consequently could devote little time to the Fund. The collective briefings were thus of distinct service to them, giving them an opportunity of listening to what the Fund had to say, of questioning its spokesmen, and of hearing the remarks of their colleagues. The discussions at such sessions were often much franker than would have been appropriate at sessions of intergovernmental bodies and led to better knowledge of Fund affairs.

These relationships, moreover, represented a two-way street. From the Mission officers we got early warnings of misunderstandings and criticisms, and were in a position to dispel the former and correct conditions leading to the latter far more quickly than if we waited until they surfaced in official interchanges. I should emphasize that in all these contacts with Mission officers, collective or individual, there was no question of seeking to influence their decisions even if, which I very much doubt, it would have been possible to do.

A whole series of these Mission officers worked hard on Fund affairs. They familiarized themselves with the Fund's programme. They gave us their advice. They supported us in debates in committee and council meetings and they helped us to avoid potentially dangerous confrontations. That I mention only a few is attributable only to editorial constraints: L. Joseph of Australia, H. Kjeldgaard of Denmark, H. O. Neuhoff of the Federal Republic of Germany, A. N. Abhyankar and A. Ghose of India, T. Hutagalung of Indonesia, Ajit Singh of Malaysia, H. Gajentaan of Netherlands, R. Gates of New Zealand, J. Arvesen of Norway, H. Mehdi of Pakistan, L. Verceles of the Philippines, I. Hamid of the Sudan, M. Stroje-Wilkens and H. Granqvist of Sweden, A. Hachani of Tunisia, J. E. C. Macrae of the United Kingdom, and S. Mousky and L. Emerson of the United States.

Other government officials who were in constant communication with the Fund included the representatives of bilateral aid programmes. Notable among these were Carl Wahren of the Swedish International Development Agency (SIDA) and Harriet Crowley and Ray T. Ravenholt of the United States Agency for International Development (USAID)—heads of the oldest and most prominent population aid programmes. It is to their credit that they have never let their bilateral interests interfere with their roles as donors to a multilateral programme.

Though the dialogue with countries participating in the Fund's programme took up much of my time, I still endeavoured to keep in touch with the representatives of countries who had reservations about population activities and consequently about the operations of the Fund itself. I found to my surprise that even the delegates from countries who opposed government-sponsored family planning programmes were eager to keep themselves informed and, when possible, to participate in other aspects of population work. This was particularly true when it came to Juan Eduardo Fleming of Argentina and Mauro Couto of Brazil who, when population matters came up in legislative bodies, took part in the debates with positive points and were careful not to infringe on the rights of other countries which wished to avail themselves of the Fund's services.

The support of the countries of eastern Europe I held to be of utmost importance for the attainment of our goal of universality and for the contribution they could make in advancing knowledge and technology. Hungary, Romania and Yugoslavia were early participants. Relations with the USSR were built up over a period of time. One of my first Mission calls was made to Ambassador M. Makeyev, Deputy Permanent Representative to the United Nations, to inform myself on the Soviet position in regard to population and to present the case of the Fund as an extension of the economic and social cooperation being offered by the United Nations to developing countries. Ambassador Makeyev expressed interest in population matters. In the meantime the Soviet Representative on the Population Commission, P. G. Podyadchikh, and the Ukrainian Representative, V. Burlin, advanced a number of ideas which were of considerable value in formulating overall policy in that they articulated a relationship between population and economic development and the part women could play in obtaining a more rationalized society. To this extent the Soviet viewpoint had a salutary effect on helping to widen the general concept of population.

The Bucharest World Population Conference, in which the Soviet Union took an active part and joined the final consensus, gave me the opportunity of speaking with the Chairman of the USSR's Statistical Board, L. Volodarsky, and the Head of the Board's Population Department, A. A. Isupov. Our discussions mainly centred on the expertise the USSR could offer in demographic training. This dialogue was continued with Under Secretary-General Arkady Shevshenko on my return to the United Nations and with the Deputy Chief of the Department of United Nations Organizations in the Ministry of Foreign Affairs, G. Lissov, at subsequent meetings of the ECOSOC and the UNDP Governing Council.

I had always hoped that negotiations would reach a stage when the Fund could avail itself of the opportunities provided by Soviet-sponsored seminars; so I welcomed an invitation to send my Deputy, Halvor Gille, as co-Director of an interregional seminar on the "Demographic Aspects of Manpower" in Moscow in 1970. Subsequently his assistant, Akira Kusukawa, expanded these contacts with the demographic community in Moscow. More recently the members of the UNDP Governing Council were pleased to hear from Soviet delegate Lissov that the USSR, in collaboration with the Fund, was prepared to offer courses in demographic training in Moscow University to students from developing countries.

Often these liaison activities had very specific purposes. It is one of my operational maxims that if there is a little spark of trouble, pour a gallon of water on it right away. Accordingly, I have tried to train my staff to sense incipient problems in both political and substantive areas.

An example of this kind of activity occurred on the eve of the first meeting of the Governing Council at which our affairs were to be considered. I heard that a senior ambassador to the United Nations did not fully understand the Fund's programme in his country and planned to deliver a speech based on information obtained from other sources. At 8.30 the next morning our Projects Division Chief, Nafis Sadik, resplendent in her sari, and I were on his doorstep to explain our policy of neutrality and responsiveness and to elaborate on his Government's request to us. The Ambassador's references to UNFPA later that day were entirely good humoured and fair.

Another type of problem occurred when a representative of a

development assistance organization of one of our major donors stationed in Bangkok became incensed with us for not funding a project which he felt was vital for the region. He wrote us an indignant letter providing us with much more information and we in turn decided that the project was worthy of support. Before the confirmatory news could arrive I happened to be passing through Bangkok and went immediately to his office and gave him the happy decision. He was flabbergasted: "My God, I did not expect you personally to bring me an answer to my letter."

At Home on a Plane

My travel schedules increased enormously in 1970-1. I had already made an intensive tour of Latin America to see at first hand what was happening in the field offices of the UNDP. I then visited a number of the university population study centres in the United States and elsewhere with the dual purpose of learning what they were doing and, through my appearances before them, making their faculty and students aware of the Fund and its operations. All had students of many nationalities who were soon to return to their respective countries to play important roles in their national population programmes.

My travels in 1972-3 were largely concerned with discussing programming matters with developing countries and signing country agreements with them. Except for two, I signed all our country agreements. Sometimes agreements were signed without even staying overnight in the country. Sometimes they were celebrated with a banquet, sometimes with a cup of coffee. Sometimes they were signed in a palace, sometimes in a director's office. Sometimes internal quarrels left the place of signing uncertain until the last minute. Once a small skirmish broke out between two departments in a government on the issue. I always hoped this was solved by my presence as an Under Secretary-General of the major world organization devoted to peace keeping.

I also visited the principal donor capitals to meet the people there interested in our affairs, to tell them of our operations and our plans, and to answer their questions. We were greatly aided in our efforts to explain our work to them by the fact that it fell within the general pattern of UNDP and the United Nations system activity with which they were already acquainted.

During this period I took part in an important series of meetings at Bellagio in the north of Italy, held under the aegis of the Rockefeller Foundation, in its impressive villa on the shore of beautiful Lake Como. These meetings were attended by many of the principal figures in population matters from various parts of the world. They discussed broad questions concerning the most useful directions population assistance efforts might take and the division of labour among major institutions in the field. Many of this group had favoured the establishment of UNFPA in the first place and were very supportive of its increasing role in international population affairs.

CHAPTER 5

Institutionalization

After two years we could say that our fundraising had been highly successful. We had reached our $15 million goal for 1970 and had received contributions of $28 million for 1971 with the prospect of more for 1972. The Netherlands and Norway had entered the list of our very substantial contributors. By the end of 1972 some fifty-six countries, mostly from the developing world, had pledged us a cumulative total of $79 million. This represented a phenomenal growth rate for any organization, let alone one within the United Nations system.

I had fully appreciated the advantages of UNFPA initially being a Trust Fund of the Secretary-General. We had been immensely fortunate in having the guidance of U Thant in the formative period and Kurt Waldheim, who had recently succeeded him, had shown serious interest in population. Nevertheless, by late 1971 I felt that the amount of public money we were handling would soon be simply too large to be managed in any way other than under the direct supervision of an official intergovernmental body, i.e. made up of representatives of governments who could provide the necessary policy orientation and guidance. Moreover, I felt that the Fund's openness to all sorts of programmes, its assistance, for example, to the sub-Sahara African countries wanting to hold censuses, and its willingness to help with programmes to increase fertility in countries that felt they had a sterility problem, had won many backers. The good missionary work of our Advisory Board and all the shoe leather and airplane tickets we had expended had also not been in vain. I estimated that by the time we could get an intergovernmental body we would have sufficient support around the globe to be able to get along with it. Some of the staff had misgivings at the idea. But after all I was the one who had done the most talking to the governments of developed, developing, Catholic and socialist countries, and trusted my own judgement.

In reaction to the growing status of the Fund, in December 1971 the General Assembly passed a resolution[1] noting that the Fund had become a "viable entity in the United Nations system" and stated its conviction "that the Fund should play a leading role in the United Nations system in promoting population programmes ...". Since the words of inter-governmental bodies, especially those of ECOSOC and the General Assembly, make a difference and open many doors in the United Nations system, this represented a major advancement for the Fund. It also went part way toward according the Fund the clearly recognized legal status which I felt that it had to have. But more was still needed.

The Fund's work and its staff were growing rapidly. It was important for us to expose our affairs to competent outside observers and get the best advice available. We had already had a consultant from Johns Hopkins University and a team of consultants from the University of North Carolina, both institutions with substantial competence in population matters. Our aim was to get all the help we could and to make the system function efficiently under its rapidly growing workload. Now I believed it was a good time to seek additional, more broadly-based advice.

These feelings of mine were at least partly reflected in the formulation of the balance of the General Assembly resolution. The operative paragraphs requested:

"the Secretary-General, in consultation with the Administrator of the United Nations Development Programme and the Executive Director of the United Nations Fund for Population Activities to take the necessary steps to achieve the desired improvements in the administrative machinery of the Fund aimed at the efficient and expeditious delivery of population programmes, including measures to quicken the pace of recruiting the experts and personnel required to cope with the increasing volume of requests, as well as to consider the training of experts and personnel in the developing countries."

This gave us, at the beginning of 1972, the opportunity we needed to set in train a course of events which led one year later to the Fund getting a formal governing body. In consultation with Paul Hoffman I decided that the way to accomplish this would be to have an authoritative group go over our affairs from head to toe and make recommendations. It could

[1] General Assembly Resolution 2815 (XXVI) (14 December 1971).

not miss, I felt, our need for more secure juridical underpinnings.

To lead this group we needed someone of ability and stature. In such circumstances I tend to look for the ablest and the most independent-minded even to the point of being critical. Ernst Michanek, the Director-General of the Swedish International Development Authority (SIDA), was an outstanding choice on both counts. Indeed, I had been anxious to get him for our Advisory Board and had not yet had a chance to accomplish this. Problems were posed by this fact and by the tight time schedule for getting the group appointed, its work done, and its report in the hands of Secretary-General Waldheim in time for him to report to the next General Assembly in September 1972. Clearly it would be appropriate for the group to be a subcommittee of our Advisory Board. But this was not going to meet until early in the spring.

Thanks to the good will and tolerance of all concerned, we were able to cut procedural corners. Michanek was chosen as the leader of the group. We helped him to select a small secretariat and the other members of the group itself. Then, with infinite politeness, the Advisory Board in the spring of 1972 called on its new member and his colleagues to do the job they had already begun. The Chairman of our Advisory Board, Alberto Lleras Camargo, deserves our thanks in connection with the successful carrying off of this shotgun wedding.

The Review Committee under Michanek's chairmanship included Lleras Camargo, Lord Caradon, Soleiman Huzayyin, John D. Rockefeller 3rd, B. R. Sen, and Turkia Ould Daddah.

We then arranged for the Review Committee to enlist Dr. George Brown of the Canadian-sponsored International Development Research Centre as head of a small staff. Brown, who was Chief of the Population and Health Sciences Division, brought another Canadian, Wendy Dobson with him. Stanley Johnson, an Englishman who had played an important role in the previously discussed US/UNA Report, Altan Unver of Turkey, and Edward Trainer of the United States completed the unit. This nearly overfulfilled our norm as regards the Review Committee's critical approach and meant that we had to treat the group with some circumspection.

We were prepared for some harsh comments and probably some uncomfortable recommendations as a result of the objective viewing we had brought upon ourselves. But I wanted the end results to be a constructive assessment and believed the Fund should have a say.

However, I felt that we should keep our comments on as narrow grounds as possible because the people most involved in the investigation had strong views on how development assistance should be delivered. I did not want to enter into what could have been a distracting controversy with those in whose hands the organizational shape of the Fund momentarily rested.

My strategy of giving the floor to others and keeping in the background in this case was the cause of some uneasiness. The Review Committee staff and Michanek, who were now deep in the investigation, expected me to put forward my system of managing aid delivery, complete with detailed long-range plans. All they got from me was a restatement of such basic UNFPA principles as policy neutrality and programming flexibility. Consequently they felt I was not providing sufficient direction to our programmes. It was only later that they understood that the type of responsiveness to countries I wanted in UNFPA could only be achieved at the cost of some explicitness in our internal operations. This was a corollary to my belief that a detailed programme plan derived from a specific country model would not be acceptable to developing countries.

Fortunately Michanek and Brown agreed with the overall policies of the Fund and decided that on balance our managerial environment was conducive to the sort of innovative work they favoured. The incident, however, illustrated what up to that time had been a slightly ironic misconception of the Fund. Some who praised us for following the wishes of the developing countries also criticized us for not imposing detailed strategies on those responsible for their country's programmes.

The Review Committee and its staff worked hard and held endless conversations and hearings both at Headquarters and in the field, going in detail and at first hand into every aspect of the Fund's work. With no little inconvenience to the individual members, the Committee finished its task and delivered a very carefully worked out report to the Secretary-General in time for him to assess it and use it as the basis for a report to the General Assembly towards the end of 1972.

A number of useful recommendations were made by the Review Committee, among them that the Fund should place a new emphasis on country planning and seek to establish more direct relationships with countries, and to this end rapidly develop its own field staff; that wherever feasible and appropriate, countries themselves should be able to directly manage the project components of country programmes financed by the Fund; that countries should have available to them as wide a choice of potential participating organizations, whether inside or outside the United Nations system, as possible; and that the Fund should have a collective guarantee by donor governments of a certain volume of future programming commitments.

These points reflected the thinking of UNFPA staff members who testified before the Review Committee and followed the lines which I hoped that the Committee would take. Indeed many of them hardly diverged from our original Policies and Procedures paper of 1969. They were eventually, very officially, embodied in an ECOSOC resolution 1763 (LIV) of 18 May 1973 which set the terms of reference for the Fund and its work.

We were at last on the right track in our efforts to let countries have the principal voice in determining the assistance they were to get and in carrying out Fund-supported projects. At the same time the Fund still had full freedom to use the very considerable skills of the United Nations, the Regional Economic Commissions, and other organizations in the system.

So far so good. But there was another aspect of the Review Committee's work which was not so easily settled. One of the objectives in arranging for the Review Committee's study was to get an intergovernmental governing board. We had hoped that the Review Committee would carry out the necessary preliminary consultations and make clear recommendations to this effect. On this point they came up with the sole inconclusive recommendation of the otherwise incisive report. It was to the effect that UNFPA should remain as a Secretary-General's Trust Fund, and "report annually to the Governing Council of the UNDP and to the Secretary-General for further reporting to the Economic and Social Council. . . . The Secretary-General should reconstitute a UNFPA Board composed of individuals selected for the contribution they can make in giving guidance to the leadership of the Fund." This could have led to the Fund still being without inter-governmental supervision.

Under these circumstances there was nothing to do but to raise the matter with Secretary-General Waldheim so that in his report to the General Assembly he might consider alternative recommendations.

While UNFPA needed an intergovernmental governing body, I was not sure about the desirable nature and locus of this body. The idea of a separate governing board which would report directly to ECOSOC, in this respect like that of UNICEF, had considerable attraction since governments could then appoint persons particularly knowledgeable in population matters to represent them.

Total independence was in principle attractive, but I doubted if it was really available. The choice seemed to be between being in the orbit of UNDP or in that of the United Nations Secretariat. Undoubtedly our affinities were more with the UNDP. It was important that population assistance should be clearly related to other economic and social development assistance, most of which in the United Nations system was already under the supervision of the UNDP Governing Council. Moreover, it was very advantageous for UNFPA to continue to avail itself of the services of the UNDP Resident Representatives in the field and to maintain close operational and policy coordination with UNDP. It might have been hard to do this if the Fund were to have a different governing body from UNDP. After much thought and discussion with Fund staff members and with the strong support of some of the major donors, I suggested to the Secretary-General that he might wish to recommend that the Fund be put under the UNDP Governing Council.

A further serious consideration remained. Some developing countries were likely to have reservations about these arrangements because they felt closer to ECOSOC than the Governing Council. They had a larger majority in ECOSOC and occasionally complained about donor domination in the Governing Council. I hoped, however, that the fact that the Governing Council functions under the supervision of ECOSOC would accommodate their point of view. ECOSOC could, after all, oversee the work of the Governing Council more closely in our case than in UNDP's if it wished to do so.

The outcome of all this was that the Secretary-General, after careful consideration, recommended to the General Assembly that the UNFPA should be placed under the supervision of the UNDP Governing Council—much to the satisfaction of two of the most articulate and active supporters of the Fund, Inga Thorsson of Sweden and John Mcdonald of the United States. The developing countries accepted the Secretary-General's recommendation and then made their point about the overall policy control of ECOSOC very explicit in the General Assembly's decision.[2]

[2] General Assembly Resolution 3019 (XXVII) (18 December 1972).

This Resolution put UNFPA "under the authority of the General Assembly", thus ending its status as a Trust Fund of the Secretary-General and enhancing its stature in the United Nations system. Then "without prejudice to the overall responsibilities and policy functions of the Economic and Social Council" and "taking into account the separate identity [of the Fund]" the Resolution said that "the Governing Council of the United Nations Development Programme, subject to the conditions to be established by the Economic and Social Council, shall be the governing body of the United Nations Fund for Population Activities". It invited the Governing Council "to concern itself with the financial and administrative policies relating to the work programme, the fundraising methods and the annual budget of the Fund". On these matters, UNFPA was to report directly to the Governing Council, "in consultation with the [UNDP] Administrator".

Just in case anyone might miss the first two times the Resolution had mentioned the policy control of ECOSOC, several developing countries insisted it be referred to once more in the balance of the resolution. Let me advance in time for a moment to explain how ECOSOC exercised this control and how the UNFPA achieved, at last, formal terms of reference which were even more favourable than those that UNFPA had made up for itself.

Terms of Reference

ECOSOC's handling of the provision of the General Assembly Resolution that the Governing Council would supervise the Fund "subject to conditions to be established by the Economic and Social Council" was highly constructive. An appropriate item was put on the agenda of the 1973 spring session and the Fund prepared a report to the Council which included a statement of the terms of reference under which we had been operating. These were somewhat less inclusive and authoritative than the aims and purposes which had been proposed for the Fund by the Michanek Committee. I had had to decide which version to recommend to ECOSOC.

While I preferred the language of the Michanek Committee, I reasoned that the old terms of reference were good enough: we had been working with them satisfactorily for some years. If we put them forward, and one or more Council members were to suggest that the Michanek version should be used instead, there would probably be enough support to approve the new terms. If, on the other hand, we ourselves were to put forward the new, more aggressive version and if any members were to object and suggest that the original version was more appropriate, one could not tell what would happen. The impression would be left, however, that some members felt that the Fund's performance did not justify the authority which the Michanek Committee had recommended.

Happily the draft resolution, which was put forward by Malaysia, used the language of the Michanek Committee and this served as the basis for the version used in the final ECOSOC Resolution 1763 (LIV). Thanks to the effective diplomacy of Ajit Singh, Counsellor of the Malaysian Mission to the United Nations, the resolution was co-sponsored by an unusually strong and representative group of countries: Ghana, Haiti, Indonesia, Madagascar, Malaysia, Mali, the Philippines, Romania, Sri Lanka, Turkey, and Uganda. It passed by a vote 22 to 0 with 5 abstentions.

Thus for the first time the Fund had terms of reference approved by an authoritative intergovernmental body. As these are still the formal terms of reference of the Fund, I am giving them in full:

"(a) To build up, on an international basis, with the assistance of the competent bodies of the United Nations system, the knowledge and the capacity to respond to national, regional, interregional and global needs in the population and family planning fields; to promote coordination in planning and programming, and to cooperate with all concerned;

"(b) To promote awareness, both in developed and in developing countries, of the social, economic and environmental implications of national and international population problems; of the human rights aspects of family planning; and of possible strategies to deal with them, in accordance with the plans and priorities of each country;

"(c) To extend systematic and sustained assistance to developing countries at their request in dealing with their population problems; such assistance to be afforded in forms and by means requested by the recipient countries and best suited to meet the individual country's needs;

"(d) To play a leading role in the United Nations system in promoting population programmes and to coordinate projects supported by the Fund."

This was very gratifying. Paragraph (a) gave us a leadership role going beyond the United Nations system. Paragraph (b) was a strong statement of our role in promoting awareness of population matters despite a few grumblings that we should be given no "normative" functions. Moreover, the scope of our role in this respect was extended to developed as well as developing countries. In paragraph (c) we had at last officially what we had been looking for all the time: a way of relating ourselves directly to recipient countries so that their wishes might be paramount in prescribing the nature and the means of our assistance.

The latter point the Council considered to be of such importance that it restated it in different form in a second operative paragraph stating that ECOSOC "Decides that the United Nations Fund for Population Activities should invite countries to utilize the most appropriate implementing agents for their programmes, recognizing that the primary responsibility for implementing rests with the countries concerned." And paragraph (d) confirmed the position the Fund had been gradually assuming within the United Nations system.

The Governing Council

My satisfaction at the practically painless acquisition of a governing body which would relieve me of many heavy responsibilities such as being the custodian and sole dispenser of large sums of public money, was further re-inforced by the thought that I now had an intergovernmental Council which could advise and guide me on the future directions of the Fund.

Up to this point we had coasted along almost totally engaged in raising money and making project commitments with as much sagacity as we could muster. The relative simplicity of our procedures, our newness, and our lack of controlling authority had the desirable effect of giving us plenty of programming flexibility and allowing us to be innovative in trying out new techniques and adopting new ideas.

Moreover, the rapid growth of the Fund had enabled us to spread out in all directions, to launch new programmes, and to answer requests of governments sometimes in as short a time as it took a cable to reach their capital cities.

But now we had a substantial enterprise in hand. Fundraising and programming were not enough. We had to follow up on project implementation, coordinate field activities, evaluate our programmes, and face up to the fact that the day was not far distant when demands might outstrip resources and we would have to set priorities. We needed the advice and guidance of a body that was truly representative of our donors and recipients, of the six great continents of the world, and of the various countries within them. This I welcomed. I would have been less than human, however, if I had not been somewhat apprehensive lest the new legislative constraints would result in a fatal rigidity.

Once again the Fund was faced with a balancing act—now a familiar challenge to us. On one side we wanted the legitimacy and the authority the Council could give us. On the other, we wanted to avoid any ties that would slow our progress and prevent us from being immediately responsive to government wishes.

Fortunately, the arrangements made by the General Assembly, ECOSOC, and the Governing Council late in 1972 and in 1973, establishing the Fund's new position and the means by which it was to be supervised by ECOSOC and the Governing Council, still left the Fund a wide operating margin. The hard work, good will, and understanding that went into formulating these arrangements on the part of many officials in home governments and on the staffs on the permanent missions to the United Nations were impressive and should be noted by those who sometimes doubt the United Nations ability to act constructively. Even more significant was the fact that those involved in these efforts understood that in an international programme in this difficult field useful actions stand by themselves and are in no way marred by a setting of some indeterminancy and inexplicitness.

The Fund's first appearance before the Governing Council was in January 1973. I gave a factual account of the Fund's overall position, presented a modest four-year resources projection, and asked the Council to permit the Fund to adopt the principles of annual funding as a means of improving planning, programming, and implementation. To grant this request was the Council's first authoritative action in regard to the Fund.

The Fund was thus able to abandon full funding principles under which all project commitments for future years must be held against current resources, a procedure we had found to be unduly restrictive. Full funding of projects at the time they were approved had advantages in the early years when the level and availability of the Fund's resources were uncertain. Under this arrangement, financial support of individual projects was assured for their duration. But it did not take account of modifications and adjustments or cancellations of projects during implementation. It also locked up money for periods of four or five years which could well be used for other undertakings. Annual funding solved these problems in that project allocations were made usually on a yearly basis.

A related innovation, which the Fund introduced in January and the Council approved at the following June session, was a "rolling plan" scheme under which the Fund would present annually a four-year Work Plan setting forth anticipated resources and expenditures for the whole period, as well as a request, based on the Work Plan, for approval authority to cover only the financial commitments the Fund expected to make during the coming year. This permitted the Council to grant further approval authority a year later on the basis of performance and on annual revision of the Work Plan.

In regard to the field programme, the Council requested the Fund to submit to it for approval three types of projects: those with a total value exceeding $1 million, comprehensive country programmes, and those which I considered innovative or having major policy implications. Pre-project expenditures were authorized in respect to such undertakings in order to avoid holdups in getting started while waiting for the next Council session. The Executive Director was permitted to take decisions on all other projects, consulting with the UNDP Administrator on those involving expenditures over $250,000.

Finally, the Council asked us to prepare, and then subsequently approved, the UNFPA Financial Rules and Regulations. Although they were closely patterned after those of UNDP, we were able to codify in them some of our departures from traditional technical assistance programme approaches, such as the "rolling plan", the right to arrange for the execution of projects by recipient governments and other agencies rather than solely by organizations of the United Nations system, and the dropping of the usual requirement that recipient governments make counterpart contributions for every project.

These arrangements in our planning, programming, and administrative processes served to institutionalize much of our fundraising efforts, letting donor countries participate in the planning and programming of resources they were providing. In addition they also gave a solid foundation for future operations.

CHAPTER 6

Building the Structure

The growth and rapid evolution of the Fund's programme necessitated constant attention to the internal shape of the Organization. In 1970, 1972, and 1974 we undertook partial reorganizations of our Headquarters structure. The main purposes were to: increase our expertise in project appraisal, provide for, and then improve monitoring and evaluation, develop planning and policy formulation functions, and take on increased administrative responsibilities resulting from the early Governing Council decisions.

The most basic reorganization took place in 1972 and is still pretty much in place. We have two Divisions and a few support units. The Projects Division is responsible, at the Headquarters level, for the development and appraisal of project proposals and the monitoring of approved projects. It is headed by Dr. Nafis Sadik, a physician from Pakistan who, as Director-General of the Family Planning Council and a member of the Planning Commission, had an important role in the development of the Pakistan family planning programme. Recently she received the Hugh Moore Award for her contribution to the family planning field. Her Division is divided into geographic sections, now headed by Joep van Arendonk, a Dutch sociologist; Roushdi El Heneidi, an Egyptian economist; José Donayre, a physician and former Executive Director of the Peruvian Centre for Population and Development Studies; Lamine N'Diaye, a Senegalese demographer who came to us from the United Nations Population Division, and Shigeaki Tomita, a Japanese economist. Finally, Paul Micou, an American lawyer with a background in project financing of development programmes, who is a Deputy Chief of this Division, along with Dr. Donayre, looks after our growing field staff requirements.

The Programme Planning Division has several major functions. The Technical Services Section, headed by A. Thavarajah, a demographer from Sri Lanka who had previously worked at the United Nations-sponsored Cairo Demographic Centre, contains population specialists charged with keeping our staff informed of new developments and trends in population matters and formulating UNFPA operating policies for inclusion in our *UNFPA Policies and Procedures Manual.* An important activity of this section is to attend to the staff work for *ad hoc* meetings of experts convened to discuss the multitude of intricate substantive and operational issues with which we must deal.

The Planning Section, headed by an American, Marion O'Connor, formerly with the Princeton University Office of Population Research, is responsible for pulling together into the UNFPA Work Plan the information we receive on future programme possibilities. The third section, added in late 1972 and headed by Jürgen Sacklowski from the Federal Republic of Germany, formerly an administrator of development assistance with a legal background, is responsible for evaluating our programmes. The first Chief of the Division was an Indian, C. Chandrasekaran, the former President of the International Union for the Scientific Study of Population, who was with the Fund from 1972 to 1974. Thavarajah is now the Acting Chief.

In addition to the Divisions there are three other sections and one unit. Edward Gregory, an American, who was formerly a public administration consultant to several governmental organizations, is responsible for administrative and financial matters, which includes overseeing the Fund's computerized financial management system. He is also responsible for our well-stocked reference library. I place particular value on the library and strongly encourage all staff to use it freely. Early in the programme, a British journalist, Ellen Ferguson, came from running the Press Section of the UNDP to build up the Fund's Information Section, which was later greatly expanded for World Population Year. The third section, headed by S. L. Tan, formerly chargé d'affaires of the Singapore Mission to the United Nations, deals with matters concerning the Fund's official relations with governments, which include the General Assembly, ECOSOC, Governing Council, and many other committees. Just to give a hint of the complexity of this United Nations system, let me list the initials of the committees with which we regularly deal: IACC, ACABQ, WGAFM, PWG,

IACB, BFC and ACC (with its preparatory committee and subsidiary bodies). Finally, to facilitate internal communications flow, we have a second small unit headed by Edward Trainer, a management specialist.

To help manage our increasingly complex operations and free me for representational and fundraising work, I recruited in 1974 a second Deputy Executive Director, C. Hart Schaaf. Schaaf, an American political scientist from the University of Michigan, came to us after 25 years of experience in running international assistance programmes in Asia, which followed a tenure as a professor of administration at Cornell University. As part of his Asian experience he spent ten years as Executive Agent of the multinational programme to develop the Lower Mekong Basin and in 1966 was a co-recipient with the Mekong Committee of a Ramon Magsaysay Award for International Understanding. He has also served as UNDP Resident Representative in three countries.

At the end of 1974, including both professional and general service staff, there were a total of 86 people from 36 nations at our New York headquarters. In addition there were 21 Coordinators from 12 nations in the field. They were responsible for a programme which had allocated a cumulative total of $168 million. The median age of the professional headquarters staff was 37, well below average in the United Nations system. Also 30 per cent were women—well above the average. Our administrative budget, which includes payment to UNDP for various financial and personnel services, remained below 7 per cent of our authorized programme level—an extremely low figure in our business.

To outsiders, and even to members of the Fund's advisory groups, it sometimes appeared that the Fund was always reorganizing. There were three contributory factors. The first was the basic functions and objectives of UNFPA. The second was the need to balance the pressures for increased rationalization of our work against those for maintaining our ability to move quickly and flexibly. The third was my own determination not to finalize decisions until I had a consensus.

It must always be remembered that UNFPA differs greatly from national or private development assistance organizations, which have specific objectives on the basis of which explicit policy can be framed. However desirable such arrangements might be for others, they were not right for the Fund. To begin with, our terms of reference were general. Then we were a creature of governments, each of which having its own philosophy and approach to population matters. The only tenable position was to encourage governments to formulate their own policies and to match the Fund's programme as closely as possible to their wishes. As the "wishes" were constantly evolving this called for a certain fluidity in approach.

To establish smooth running operations under such circumstances took time and readjustments.

Freedom and order both had their proponents among the UNFPA staff. I let these two forces struggle with one another and guided the way they did. Seeking contradictory objectives at the same time worries me much less than some administrators. Perhaps this is because in Asia one is used to the "yin" and the "yang" as opposing but legitimate aspects of the same thing.

In gradual concessions to the forces for order I agreed to increasingly stringent requirements in reporting on expenditures and the status of project implementation, on project budgeting, on forward planning, and in preparing documents for the Governing Council. For instance, in late 1972 we began to use a computerized financial information system for all our projects.

All project budgetary commitments, divided into annual segments, are entered into this system. Expenditures incurred against the commitments are also entered into the computer and periodic reports of allocations and the subsequent expenditures are produced. The system is the basic financial record link between the Fund and the organizations which implement our programmes. It is designed so that financial commitments in our programme cannot exceed our annual approval authority. The financial data processed by the computer is also used as a data bank for various analyses of the UNFPA Work Plan and programme. Data on rates of implementation, types of inputs (personnel, training, equipment), distribution of the programme geographically and by Work Plan category are some of the regular analyses which are made.

We also reformulated or codified our existing policies and procedures into a Manual. The Manual, a looseleaf notebook, contains sections on the Fund's organization structure, major policies, operating procedures, financial regulations and rules, administrative and personnel procedures, and field operations.

Finally, I established our Evaluation Section. Its purpose has been to develop a process of independent evaulations in the form of in-depth analyses of UNFPA programmes. The findings have determined the degree to which projects have achieved their objectives and, even more important, what factors were the major obstacles in the operations of the project. The insights gained through this process have improved the Fund's programming skills.

In deference to the advocates of freedom I avoided imposing a rigid programme budget as long as the balance between demand and resources could be achieved by severe screening for quality. I also constantly stressed the continued need for programming flexibility and speed.

The third factor contributing to the continuously evolving UNFPA structure has been my interest in not finalizing decisions until there is a consensus. To explain this element of my personal style let me pause for a few moments to summarize my overall management approach.

Management Approach

To build an organization which would be responsive to widely divergent constituencies and capable of providing leadership for an effective worldwide population programme was to me a most fascinating kind of challenge, one which was an important motivation for my coming to UNFPA in the first place. To this task I brought a management style which had evolved both from my experience in the Philippines and through my studies of management literature.

My approach is first to become familiar with the people with whom I will be cooperating. I have made it a personal routine to learn as much as possible about the background of the people with whom I am going to be in contact whether they are staff members, government officials, or heads of organizations. For example, in meeting officials from countries I am not personally acquainted with, I keep in mind that the panoplies of power and statehood often tend to conceal the personalities behind the facade. Therefore, I prepare myself by reading as much as I can about their country. These readings give me a glimpse of the totality of where they come from and ensures that from the start I am on the same wavelength as the officials to whom I am talking.

In the culture in which I grew up, interpersonal communication is a highly cultivated art. We take account of the total personality of the individual in all its complexity even when it comes to business relationships. The importance of this was recognized by the Swedish economist Gunnar Myrdal in an Allport Memorial Lecture at Harvard University when he said: "We are dealing with the behaviour of human beings, each of whom has a soul, and is influenced by his living conditions in the widest sense of the word. These vary widely and change all the time, as does their relationship to behaviour."

By making every effort to know the people with whom I work and their behavioural tendencies, and to understand their points of view, I am better able to understand the fundamental issues involved in a problem situation. Of course, the predominantly political constituents of UNFPA further encouraged me to be "people-oriented". Some, for example, are representatives of member states and yet tend to mix their official positions with their individual views. To communicate with them, I find it essential to know the relative weights of the two.

My focus on people does not mean that I do not consider ideas important. I try vigorously to understand these first. Nor does this mean that I do not study the formal statements and documents in which these ideas are expressed. I pay equal attention to them too. But over and above them, in attempting to seek or make a decision, I must know who says what, when, how, and even why he says it.

Emphasis on people as the central element of any problem has been criticized as unnecessary and unscientific. But this criticism has never been totally justified and is fast diminishing in the current management literature. Managing a United Nations agency, moreover, is quite different from running a business enterprise. It often happens that the primary clients of the Fund—the recipient countries—are not just clients but also members of its board of directors. This client-board member relation is not a feature of the private business sector. In the United Nations system the implementation of a project ultimately rests with a sovereign government over whose decisions we have, of course, no authority. Thus, good communications become all important.

By constantly linking people with their ideas it became easier for me to identify those who will be affected by the outcome of a possible decision and to anticipate how they would react. I then try to involve in the decision making all those to be affected regardless of their formal organizational position. An individual thereafter has a part in the ultimate decision even when it has been reached on the basis of an initially small area of consensus among the participants. The extent to which his own points surface will determine his resulting behaviour. If he feels that the decision is partly his own, he will be more willing to carry it out than if his views had not been respected.

An example of how I have used this method in the administration of the Fund is the Management Committee. This Committee, because of the decentralized structure of the Fund, consists of all officers at the section chief level and above, numbering in all eighteen. It usually meets once a week and is the final decision-making point for most important issues. While my own points of view carry some weight in this Committee, the decisions it makes follow careful discussion and consensus formation. The Committee thus serves both as a measure of control and as a way to find a possible area of agreement leading to a decision which the staff can then carry out effectively. These decisions and the basic arguments supporting them are recorded and the minutes circulated to all the officers of UNFPA in the headquarters and the field for information or implementation.

In conducting these meetings I usually confine my role to defining the nature of the problem and stating some probable alternatives to its solution. The staff then debates the possible courses of action. I never monopolize the discussions. Habitually I limit myself to a few questions designed more to evoke clarity of thinking than to demonstrate what I know, even if, in fact, I may know more than the speaker on a particular point. I am fond of comparing my behaviour in chairing a meeting and eliciting a consensus, to a mirror. Mirrors are useful because they allow the user to see himself more clearly than his senses normally permit. It is also the main device by which persons detect their blemishes before they are noticed by others. By reflecting back accurately to the participant his ideas together with those of his colleagues, I enable him to perceive the relevance of his ideas to the problem at hand and their relationship with those of the others. In the course of the discussion, he gradually locates himself and his position in the total situation. This is what the mirror actually does—makes us more aware of realities. When the elements of consensus appear I put it in words and announce the decision.

Some initially felt that our multilevel Management Committee and its openness in discussing issues where a section chief might express a point of view different from that of his division chief, undercut their authority. It has taken time to prove that group discussion does not preclude the use of formal authority. Indeed, it often makes it easier to maintain, since the system commits subordinate unit chiefs to the overall policies of the Fund and thus takes the onus for these policies off their direct superiors. It also gives the superior a chance to show his broader grasp of issues.

For similar reasons I set up another large representative group of staff members to decide what projects the Fund should support. This Project Review Committee, as it is called, is a unique body in that its membership includes at any given meeting all those who have participated in the appraisal of a proposal, irrespective of rank, and any other interested officers.

Many points of view have to be taken into account in the Fund's decision making, and an equal amount of conflict resolved before the consensus is reached. While as a Filipino I value harmony, I realize that conflict can never be eliminated. Human beings are in a certain sense quantums of energy. If you block that energy from expression in one direction, it will invariably go off in another. Provided conflict can be contained in an acceptable framework it can be put to good use. Canalized conflict has been an important factor in the vitality of the Fund. A tighter formal structure under which people are rigidly held in administratively sealed boxes tends to crush initiative, sterilize the organization, and, what is worse, force it to become old before its time. Whatever else has happened to the Fund it has not suffered hardening of the arteries.

The participatory consensus-oriented decision-making style also requires patience and a certain degree of tolerance for ambiguity from the participants. Creativity in decision making, however, requires this tolerance—an attitude not readily found among those who have been trained in well-established bureaucracies. Yet in the end the decisions reached by consensus can be as precise as those directed unilaterally from above. They also tend to be more effective since they are better understood by the participants who, in addition, are more committed to their implementation.

This large measure of participation from the staff ensures, moreover, constant awareness of our objectives and makes UNFPA officers particularly sensitive to incipient problems. I believe in solving problems at their inception or, better yet, before, and try never to allow them to reach crisis proportions. To reinforce this attitude and allow immediate response from the Fund I have liberally delegated authority to responsible officers within the Organization. To do this without allowing the Organization to wander from the pursuit of its immediate and long-range goals requires a good understanding of one's staff and how they behave in various circumstances. As has been said, the challenge to management of this style is continuously to harmonize individual integrity with the collective continuity.

I have followed this decision-making style in both internal and external matters. Thus, despite a basic difference between my relationship with governments who direct me, and my relationship with the staff who are under my direct authority, I behave in essentially the same manner. I have in fact tried to infuse all my colleagues in the Fund with basically the same attitude. They have in turn created for themselves an organization that appears to be sensitive and well adjusted to its very complicated environment.

Personnel and Personality

Matters which I do not fully delegate include decisions on broad policies, issues liable to involve severe conflict, and personnel recruitment. Choice of personnel is critical to the success of my decision-making system. Even by seeing a candidate briefly I can often avoid mistakes. What I look for in a candidate, in addition to talent, is a reasonably well-integrated personality. Persons with basic instability or a very high degree of internal conflict can act in unpredictable ways harmful to the organization. Even if they remain stable, too high a proportion of their energies are devoted to maintaining their own stability.

A person who is not reasonably at home with himself may read malice into the actions of others even when none is present and thus become an endless source of trouble. I do not claim to be able to read vibrations and brain waves; but a person almost always gives you small clues in behaviour or speech if you are alert to catch them and not too busy talking yourself. Personnel decisions, however, often, involve trade-offs. You can sometimes afford to buy substantial problems if at the same time you get even more substantial talent. I also believe in assembling a staff with widely varying ideas and cultural backgrounds—not a difficult job in the United Nations. Variety is the spice of life. More seriously, it also helps ensure organizational creativity.

Generally, we have looked for two types of persons: first, those with professional qualifications in the academic disciplines bearing on population matters like demography, medicine, and sociology, and also with experience in population work; and, second, those with programming experience in other fields of development assistance. I believed that both were necessary. Although at first they looked askance at each other, I found them of equal and, indeed, rather similar abilities. In particular, I kept my eyes open for live wires, usually young and unconventional, and I found them. Even though I knew I was asking for constant controversy, divergences of views, and from time to time personality clashes, I was convinced that the calibre of the contestants would make them put the objectives of the Fund ahead of personal concerns. In the meantime any tendencies towards bureaucratization would have received a salutary shakeup.

I have been most encouraged to see the extent to which this multinational group with twenty-seven different languages has become a community with lasting friendships as well as developing the ability to work well together. All of us learn a great deal about other cultures by working with people from them. One gains insights into people and situations around the globe by seeing them through the eyes of the colleagues best able to understand them.

Field Staff

The Fund's field programmes come under the supervision of the UNDP Resident Representatives. The Resident Representatives head up the Field Offices of the UNDP in 106 countries and rank as the senior United Nations presence in the countries of their assignment. In the course of their duties they maintain close contacts with governments to identify over the whole span of national and economic development areas where external aid can be put to best use. They then help to draw up the assistance programmes and monitor their execution. They also act, as I said earlier, as coordinating centres for all assistance programmes in the country. The backing of these experienced officers has done much to accelerate the progress of the Fund's field programme.

With the services of this invaluable network at the Fund's disposal, we did not need to make special appointments in the field until the number of population projects in any one country or region began to place too heavy a burden on the Resident Representative and he suggested that his staff should be strengthened by the addition of a qualified population officer.

An example of how this process worked was seen in Sri Lanka in the early seventies. The Resident Representative, convinced of the need to consider population variables in economic and social development programmes, was anxious to show that a predominantly agricultural, tropical Asian country could have a successful population programme. Becoming aware of the possibility of receiving substantial funds for population projects, he, together with representatives from ILO, UNESCO, WHO, and the IPPF affiliate in Sri Lanka, began discussions with the Government concerning possible projects in several areas. With UNFPA Headquarters reacting positively to various project ideas, these discussions resulted, in early 1973, in a four-year $6 million agreement with the Government for a programme of eleven project components.

The Ministries of Planning, Health, Education, Labour, and Information and Broadcasting were associated in this multifaceted United Nations system effort requiring the annual expenditure of UNFPA funds equal to one half of the annual expenditure on the UNDP programme in the country. Major activities included expansion of the family planning delivery system within the well-developed government health system, the introduction of population subjects in the schools from the sixth grade onwards, covering every child in the country, development and implementation of various communication measures to support these programmes, and a special study of population-related laws in Sri Lanka. The latter was part of a global effort sponsored by UNFPA.

When the Agreement between UNFPA and the Government was signed, the Resident Representative had to prepare, in conjunction with the United Nations and government agencies, detailed plans of operation for the eleven projects. This placed such a heavy work load on his office that he pressed for the assignment of a UNFPA Coordinator. A UNFPA staff member with extensive academic and practical experience in population was then sent to help him.

To facilitate programme implementation, the Agreement called for the establishment of a high level governmental Project Implementation Committee. The Resident Representative sat on this Committee with representatives of the various government agencies participating in the programme. So did the Coordinator, thereby enabling him to shoulder much of the burden of monitoring programme progress and trying to solve the many problems which arise in all such cases.

The functions of the Coordinators are reasonably well described by their title. Their role is to maintain close contact, under the supervision of the Resident Representative, with the Government in order to inform officials of the support which the Fund can give and the technical assistance which is available through the United Nations system. They are also expected to ascertain the nature of the Government's needs and wishes, and to see that assistance is provided in an appropriate, timely, and effective manner.

Some Coordinators do have professional backgrounds which qualify them to give advice. I can think of one well-qualified Coordinator, a woman, who can give expert aid to the Minister of Health on the specifications of contraceptives in the morning, sort her way through the specifications of various types of data-processing equipment in the afternoon, and then in the evening report in very lucid fashion on all relevant factors to Fund Headquarters. Advice, however, is not the Coordinator's principal function. The United Nations, including UNFPA, is a system of more or less bureaucratic organizations and it is up to the Coordinator to see to it that this system works to the benefit of the particular country.

I have often been asked to define the qualifications for such an assignment. Previous administrative and field experience with development assistance programmes, is, of course, helpful. It is essential to know what it takes to get a project approved and then make it move forward. Being an intelligent and sympathetic person is also very much to the point. But getting the assistance actually delivered ranks as the priority task with both the Government and the Fund.

Two other qualifications are less tangible but extremely important. One is stature, and the other judgement. The Coordinator must be able to deal with ministers and gain their respect. This inevitably involves certain requirements of age, experience, skills, and intelligence in various combinations. The Coordinator's stature will almost surely determine the level of official allocated to deal with him in whatever ministry, usually the Ministry of Health, has the chief responsibility for population programmes. The Coordinator has to work on a day-to-day basis with the officials responsible for population work. It is also important that he have access to the relevant minister and, indeed, to other key ministers as well, like the Minister of Planning or the Minister of Finance, since the success of the population programme usually requires their support.

It is not easy to put your finger on the judgement factor in advance. However, it becomes only too clear in practice when judgement is lacking. Although a Coordinator works under the general supervision of the Resident Representative, the latter has many other concerns and almost always delegates much of the responsibility of carrying on the Fund's business to his UNFPA colleague. A Coordinator who is short on judgement can easily bring operations to an unnecessary halt by insisting on certain details of performance which might look good by the book but which under the circumstances are quite unrealistic. He can also lose the confidence of those with whom he has to deal by appearing in other ways to be more demanding or restrictive than UNFPA Headquarters. Indeed, an able Coordinator instinctively knows how to make Headquarters rather than himself look like the villain when there is need for one.

Anyone who has represented an aid organization in the field knows that the work is often onerous and frustrating, demanding real dedication and constant self-reminders of the importance of the job. Mixed in with diplomacy is much patient work in the preparation of programming documents and budgets so that the requested assistance can be approved and supplied promptly.

I asked one of our Coordinators to give me a rundown on what his job was really like. I was almost sorry I did because he related the following tale to me and I began to be conscience-stricken at what we were expecting him to do.

On his arrival in his assigned country some years ago, he played an important role in getting fifteen projects, already identified by the Government, into concrete shape, with work plans and budgets, so that they could be approved by the National Population Commission, the National Economic Development Authority, and UNFPA Headquarters, and readied for execution by the selected international and national organizations.

To do this he worked in the first instance with the National Population Commission, which was the central body charged with carrying out coordinated national population programmes and therefore the one with control over the release of all resources, domestic and foreign, flowing into the programme. In addition, he took a leading part in the arrangements with the organizations which would carry out the projects. This list included United Nations Secretariat, UNESCO, WHO, and fifteen different national organizations, some governmental, some private, among whom were the Ministries of Education, Health, Agriculture, Social Welfare, and Labour, the Bureau of Census and Statistics, a university, a Responsible Parenthood Council, and a Social Institute.

USAID was a substantial source of external assistance to this country and most of its funds flowed into a network of family planning activities in clinics throughout the country. Accordingly, in helping to develop a Fund programme, UNFPA concentrated on communication, information, and education inputs coordinated with these other efforts.

Fifteen projects in all were included in the programme. Two give some idea of the scope: the Hospital Project, with which WHO was associated, and the Population Education Project, with which UNESCO was associated. In the Hospital Project, family planning counselling services were to be extended in twenty-five hospitals and it was proposed to expand this number to one hundred. In the Population Education Project of the Ministry of Education some 200,000 teachers were to be taught to give population education in 200,000 classrooms.

The financing for these activities was channelled directly through UNDP/UNFPA channels. Thus a massive auditing job had to be done as the accounts of each of the fifteen projects had to be balanced each month. There were two locally hired employees on the UNFPA payroll in the UNDP Finance Office to accomplish this task.

Auditing, incidentally, though demanding, is the smallest part of the monitoring job which the Coordinator must get done. Much more vital is looking at the projects to see whether they are being carried out in accordance with plans, whether they make sense, whether they are actually helpful, and whether they are an integral part of broader economic and social programmes.

Even this abbreviated version of what I was told illustrates that a

Coordinator cannot perform his functions adequately away from his desk. Yet he cannot perform his functions adequately unless he does get around. In this particular case, the Coordinator solved the problem of being in several places at the same time by having both a pilot's licence and airplane. I hasten to add that the plane is his own and the pilot's licence is not a UNFPA requirement for the job.

CHAPTER 7

The Fund's Approach to Assistance

Because the United Nations system is so complex in its interdependencies and relationships, I have had to make a lot of statements to clarify its working principles and assumptions.

These operational assumptions, as the Hindus would put it, did not "spring full-blown from the navel of Brahma" upon coming to the Fund. Many of us did carry them in our heads from past "incarnations" but they were essentially developed in a continuous process of relating our formal mandates to our operations and by reflecting on our day-to-day solutions to problems. The shaping of these ideas was not an easy task. We had to be both persevering and consistent.

I had not come to the Fund from one of the specific "population" disciplines. As a consequence I did not attempt to second guess the professional insights of the demographers, statisticians, economists, sociologists, and public health specialists on the staff. But as the head of the Organization it was my task to set an overall framework and articulate these ideas in the official statements that I had to make. Perhaps, because I did not belong to the "population club", I had a colder eye in looking at our record and a less-impassioned view in doing so.

Countries are Sovereign

Before I had any contact with the United Nations the words "sovereignty", "sovereign rights", and "international relations" were terms comprehensible to me only in my academic courses and coloured by the insular needs of my country. However, as early as 1952, when I was a delegate to the UNESCO Conference on Media and Youth, I began to realize the larger significance of these terms. Twenty-three years and innumerable international meetings and assemblies later, I understood their operational content with some confidence.

It was predictable that my first public statements would be aimed at imprinting in the minds of all my co-workers the importance of the sovereign right of countries to determine their own course of action in population matters. These statements also served as a constant reminder to our donors and recipients that the Fund would respond only to a country's own assessment of its needs in population.

There is another reason for this approach. Countries see their population situations differently. After all, their position on population matters is a mix of cultural, economic, and demographic circumstances and also depends greatly on the level of sophistication and comprehensiveness with which the problem is perceived. Consequently their requests may vary from a single census advisor to a multidisciplinary action programme requiring millions of dollars. There is no single formula that all can follow.

The extent to which the Fund has conformed to these imperatives is stamped all over its programme. In Asia, for instance, over 60 per cent of the Fund's support is for family planning and related activities, while in Africa, the United Republic of Cameroon has received assistance with programmes to find the medical causes of infertility or subfertility. In all these cases the Fund's role is analogous to that of a staff function for the countries. We analyse the feasibility of the programmes requested, inform the country of our evaluation, and obtain approval of the Governing Council for major programme assistance.

Marginality of International Assistance

We have never doubted that all forms of international assistance, grants or loans, private or public, bilateral or multilateral, to developing countries are important. There are certain activities, however, that international organizations can undertake without arousing suspicion where this would not be so easy for bilateral donors. This is especially true in a highly sensitive field like population.

But international assistance, even when measured in its broadest terms, has never been more than a small addition to the total resources that recipient countries devote to their own development. This is also very apparent in the case of population. An estimate of its annual flow from developed to developing countries puts it now at around $300 million, only slightly more than 2 per cent of the total of official development assistance. Its marginality is well illustrated in the case of India. India is providing a total of $688 million in its current Five Year Plan for its population programme. This makes the Fund's projected assistance of $40 million over this period a mere 6 per cent of the total effort.

I felt very conscious of the Fund's peripheral role when I spoke with the Prime Minister of Fiji, Ratu Sir Kamisese Mara, when I called on him in Suva in 1973. After being informed that I had come to inquire about the needs of Fiji for assistance, he asked how long the United Nations had been extending aid in population to countries. I answered since 1969. With a paternal look he ardently recounted how his Government had started its population programme six years before the United Nations took cognizance of population problems, and that its target had been reached because they relied on their own resources. However, he concluded, there might be areas in the programme where international assistance would be needed. He was true to his word. Not long thereafter the Fund approved a request for assistance to their 1976 census.

The Fund has always been aware of the limitations of its effort, even with a $80 million budget for 1975. Just how much effect could such an amount have for the population programme needs of the developing world? Because we believe that our efforts are marginal, we strive to ensure that they are more than marginally effective. Economic theory teaches us that it is the addition of new resources which sets the standards of expansion—the costs, the benefits, and the productivity. It is the marginal effectiveness of each added portion of aid which is significant. The Fund therefore seeks to give priority to projects which promise the best returns in the long run. The role of population assistance in these circumstances is to act as a spur towards national effort rather than a substitute for it.

Developing Self-reliance

The Fund's operational philosophy has always been directed towards building up the capacity and ability of recipient countries to deal with, as soon as possible, their own needs. Accordingly, we have devoted a major proportion of the Fund's resources on a long-term basis to strengthen national institutions and training. However, in any given operational area we have normally restricted our assistance to a limited period of time. In the case of such types of assistance as local salary support we have used a declining scale as well.

The very act of giving these grants implies, primarily, mutual respect and concern between donors and recipients. After all, we are only the trustees of the good will that comes from both. Each commitment we make is just that—an act of trust in the administrations concerned, a declaration that we are willing to rely on their judgement of conditions and needs in their own country, and on their ability to carry through sustained population programmes. Because of this fundamental demonstration of trust at the outset we find, as the relationship proceeds, that we can make suggestions on policy as interested friends, not as creditors.

I believe with Jan P. Pronk, Minister for Development Cooperation of the Netherlands, that "the present relation between developed and developing countries leaves insufficient room for economic and social development and one of the essential elements needed to change this situation is an increased self-reliance of developing countries".

Beyond Family Planning

In the years immediately preceding my arrival in New York there was a feeling among those dealing with population matters that the General Assembly Resolution of 1966 had represented a breakthrough, that the main issues were settled, and that it remained only to take the necessary action. Although rapid population growth threatened to jeopardize the economic progress made by developing countries, the organization of national family planning programmes seemed to offer the means whereby fertility could be reduced without infringing on individual rights. Bilateral and multilateral agencies would provide the necessary assistance.

When I joined UNFPA in 1969 this feeling was still strong although there were already signs that perhaps family planning was not the total answer to the population problem. Subsequently there was a profound evolution in thinking, and the ground on which action programmes were built no longer seemed quite as sound as it had several years earlier.

One of the factors behind this was undoubtedly the lack of clear evidence that national family planning programmes were producing results quickly enough. I felt that all concerned might have expected too much too soon from family planning programmes. I suspected that the understandable urge to involve governments and the world community in action programmes as quickly as possible had led to a decision to go ahead even though the evidence and assumptions on which these programmes were based had not been clearly established.

The Second Asian Population Conference held in Tokyo, Japan, in November 1972 seemed an appropriate occasion for me to voice my own assessment in that the Asian countries were well ahead of most others in their attitudes towards family planning programmes. My theme was that we must look much beyond such programmes for effectiveness. Frankly, it raised a number of eyebrows. While emphasizing that I was not advocating the abandonment of family planning programmes but rather that they should be improved and intensified, I suggested that we deepen our understanding of the factor influencing decisions about family size as these are perceived by the people concerned. Findings in this area would make it easier to help couples in developing countries understand their predicament, for, in the final analysis, it is better understanding which is the key to action and not engineering from the outside.

In this sense I suggested much greater attention be paid to education. Education on population problems and their implications, as well as the basic principles of human reproduction and family planning, should be a key part of family life education to be provided to all children and youth. In this way future generations of prospective parents will be prepared for their responsibilities. In addition, I urged that special consideration should be given to legislation raising the legal age at marriage, increased employment opportunities for women, and general improvement of the status of women in the community. Such measures also could have a significant impact on fertility patterns.

Based on these beliefs I started widening the scope of the Fund's assistance to include many related activities as essential partners, but not, of course, substitutes for family planning programmes, which have and continue to receive about 50 per cent of the Fund's resources.

Development and Population

I became acquainted with the population problem in my country after several years of working in development programmes. Becoming the head of the Fund was in one aspect a novel experience for me in that I was now looking at the relationship of development and population from the opposite direction, with population coming first. But I had not forgotten the lessons of the past. To my mind, population programmes must be closely coordinated with the total development effort. And this should be true of external assistance as well.

The effort to develop is basically an attempt by the developing countries to eradicate the permanence of poverty in which most of their people live. This is not simply material poverty—although the *per capita* income of developing countries is only a fraction of that in the more developed—but a lack of most of the things which make life worth living, including very often, hope.

Through the years, enormous amounts of resources, some from the more developed countries, but mostly from the developing countries themselves, have been invested in development projects. The results have been a visible increase in the overall economic growth rates of the majority of developing countries. One should not underestimate their achievements in this regard. Most of them are supporting vastly increased populations. What is more famines and epidemics—regular features of life in the past—have been eliminated. In many, since the 1940s, the average life span has risen fifteen to twenty years.

But lasting improvements in the lives of the majority of the people in these countries is a goal yet to be achieved. Developing countries have an enormous potential if the untapped reserves of energy and resourcefulness of the more deprived strata could be released to productive uses. This is a difficult exercise about which the economists' original paradigms have not been very clear.

Twenty years ago, when serious development programmes were beginning in the former colonial territories, it was generally believed that what was needed was capital investment in industry which would lead to urban development along the lines laid down in Europe and North America. During the 1960s, the first Development Decade, these policies

The Muslim world is paying increasing attention to population matters. Here a religious leader explains the concept of balanced families to veiled Muslim women in the Sheikh Halouagy Mosque in Alexandria. (W.H.O.)

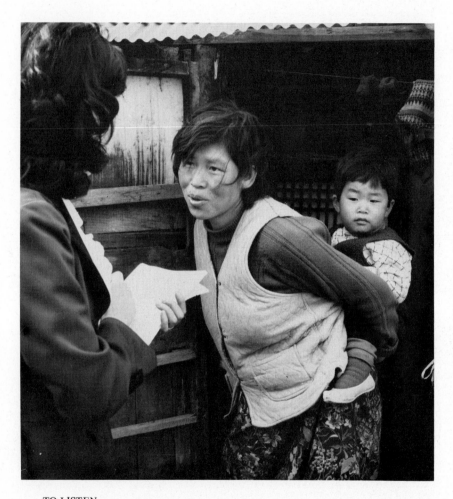

TO LISTEN . . . .
A social worker not only gives advice but seeks to add to existing population knowledge by getting the village women to recount their personal experiences of contraceptive methods. (W.H.O.)

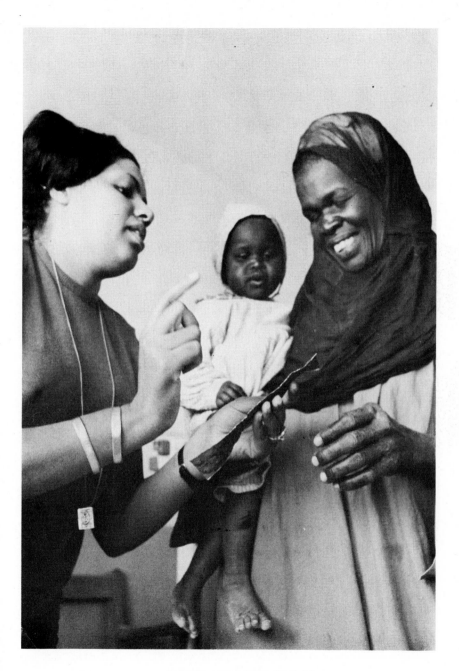

. . . . AS WELL AS TO TELL (W.H.O.)

Villages can only be reached by boat in Nong Jok, Thailand. In this [predominantly Muslim area] a female population worker talks to a man about male contraception. (I.P.P.F.)

At the World Population Conference in Bucharest in 1974 high level delegates from 136 countries reached a consensus on a worldwide population plan of action. This was the first global inter-governmental meeting to be held with population as its sole theme. (United Nations)

The family planning programme in Indonesia uses a diverse variety of teaching techniques to promote greater understanding of population. One of its most popular forms is a puppet show telling simple stories of the benefits derived from controlling family size. Puppetry is a very highly developed artistic medium in Indonesia. (W.H.O.)

Artists are also playing their part by designing posters that will attract the widest possible general attention. This photograph was taken in the Philippines. (U.N.E.S.C.O.)

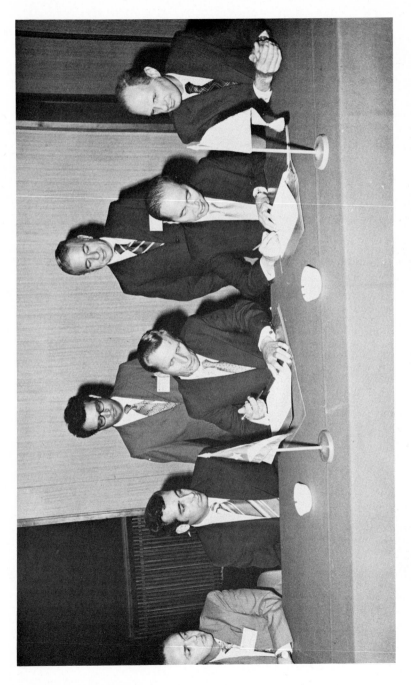

Signing in August 1974 a Project Agreement between the Government of the Republic of Cuba and the U.N.F.P.A. This was the first major Agreement between a socialist country and the U.N.F.P.A. and involves an expenditure of US$ 3.8 million over a four year period. Mr. Guttierez (third from left) and Mr. Salas signing the Agreement. (United Nations)

Having no choice gives no chance. (I.L.O.)

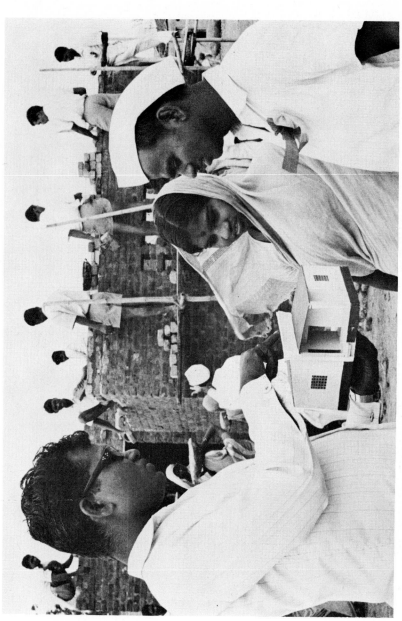

A successful experiment in social planning in which the Fund was able to assist. 56 young couples took part in pilot courses in population and family welfare education at Aurangabad, India in October 1972. In addition to population and family planning education courses were given in cooking, home economics, child care, village administration and on the work of co-operatives and trade unions. (I.L.O.)

Population census being taken in Lagos, Nigeria. (United Nations/M. Macauley).

appeared to pay off in many countries in terms of high annual rise in Gross National Product. Overall annual growth rate during the 1960s for developing countries was 5.6 per cent, a rate hardly reached by the industrialized countries at any time in their history. The Pearson Report,[1] published in 1969, pointed out phenomenal increases in the production of electricity and other forms of energy, in industrial capacity, in agricultural production, in roads, hospitals, and schools built.

There had been an optimistic theory that the benefits of this growth would, as it was put, "trickle down" through the various strata of society eventually reaching even the very poor. By the end of the first Development Decade it was clear that this was not happening. More people were poorer than ever before, and many development programmes had failed to keep up with rising populations in providing even the most basic services. In some countries, even though national wealth was rising rapidly, the proportion of wealth enjoyed by the poorer sections of the community had actually gone down.

The emphasis on rapid industrialization has led to a cult of bigness in both industry and agriculture in the belief that large units are necessarily more efficient than small ones. Small businesses have not had the same easy access to credit as larger ones. Small farmers without special assistance have not been able to take advantage of the benefits of the Green Revolution which brought advanced technology to bear on the production of food grains in developing countries.

Only slowly have we groped towards a theory which would give the majority of the people a share in growing wealth and depend on them to produce it. The key to economic growth is savings and investment. It has now been shown in countries with widely differing ideologies that it is not only the prosperous who save. Relatively poor producers and workers will save, too, if given the opportunity. But in order to do this they need to have access to health and education services; they need credit, the appropriate technology, and advice on using it. In other words the initial investment need not be in big operations, whether industrial or agricultural, but can be widely diffused over thousands of small undertakings.

---

[1] So-called because the Commission on International Development financed by the World Bank but a wholly independent effort was headed by Lester B. Pearson of Canada.

These observations on development generally coincide with the conclusion being drawn by students of population growth patterns. It has been clear that even the broadest family planning campaigns on their own are largely ineffective in producing a lower rate of population growth. Experience in a dozen different countries has shown that many other factors are also contributors to the lowering of population growth rates. These include adequate housing for all, full employment, ready access to education and health services; in other words, precisely the conditions which would prevail in an area applying the small-scale theory of development which I have suggested.

I had an opportunity to observe how this was taking shape in one country, perhaps the most significant of all, because it has the largest population—China.

At the invitation of the Government I visited the country in late 1972 and had an opportunity to discuss population problems with the officials directing the various Birth Planning Programmes in Shanghai and Peking. Vice Foreign Minister Fu Hao and An Chih-yuan, Director of the International Organizations Department, who were my official hosts, gave me a fine opportunity to observe these programmes both in the cities and in the communes.

Before the trip I knew about the policies of China on late marriages, birth spacing, and the teaching of small-family norms. But observing at first hand the manner in which these policies were worked out in the smallest political and administrative units of the country was the most instructive part of the visit.

China views its birth planning programmes as an integral part of its development efforts. Specifically, these programmes are part of the health services available to all citizens who need them. All forms of contraception from pills to sterilization are utilized. But what was interesting to me in the management of these programmes was not the wide variety of techniques employed but the emphasis given to motivating couples to make a decision on the size of their families.

This motivational work is done through formal education, neighbourhood group discussions, and even by home visits from both medical personnel and the "barefoot doctors". The message is for parents to have smaller families. Whether in factories or in communes, the couples are encouraged and assisted to make the decisions themselves on how to achieve their own birth-planning objectives. This type of participatory decision making and the skilful use of small groups strongly reminded me of the methods we used in my country to increase food production.

I left China with a feeling that I had found a really good example of how to integrate family planning programmes into development and even more significant to do all these without any external assistance at all but as a sheer act of will of both people and government. This was to influence my thinking and the Fund's.

However, no matter how impressed I was, I also wondered how much of this experience would be transferrable to other countries. I obviously could not give a satisfactory answer after such a short visit. But I was convinced that if these experiences were shared, certain approaches could be adapted by other countries. And so upon my return to New York I suggested that the Chinese Government might participate more in the population activities of the United Nations system. I repeated this appeal when replying to some remarks by the Chinese delegate in the Fund's Governing Council, in June, 1975.

Quite incidentally, when I was discussing population questions with the experts in Peking, I mentioned that in some countries there is difficulty in starting population programmes because of the Aristotelian view that the soul enters the foetus at the moment of inception. This was met with some amusement and furnished me with one more instance of how people of different cultural backgrounds think about the issues of Man's nature, birth, and death.

With the Catholics

A set of beliefs on population which were of great importance to us and to which we gave great attention were those of the Catholic Church. The present Catholic policy on population is embodied in two papal encyclicals, *Populorum Progressio (1967)* and *Humanae Vitae (1968)*, and in the Constitution *Gaudium et Spes* of the Second Vatican Council. These taken together, while acknowledging the problems of rapidly increasing population, ban all forms of artificial contraception for Catholics. This leaves periodic abstinence as the only means by which Catholics can limit births. If couples desire fewer children they have to restrict their sexual relations to the woman's infertile period measured by the use of the calendar, a specially designed thermometer, or other means.

When Pope Paul VI issued the *Humanae Vitae*, many of the experts in population were dismayed by the encyclical. To them it was a serious obstacle to the fast-spreading family planning movement in Catholic countries. The idea of linking birth limitation to the Catholic ideas on family, love, and marriage, under a movement for Responsible Parenthood, was too slack a pace for those who wanted to transform the world in a few years.

This impatience is not easily comprehensible to those who are in Catholic countries. If one looks at this policy carefully, the Church does not encourage unlimited number of births beyond the capacities of families to support. On the contrary, and this is where many miss the point, it accepts the concept of limitation. It is in the method of attaining the limitation that the argument is all about. And provided the Church is not challenged on this score it has no objection to a country adopting a population policy or having a programme. At least, this is what happened in my own country which is about 80 per cent Catholic.

When I was the Executive Secretary in the Philippines it was one of my duties to do the staff work for the Presidential Orders that incorporate executive policies on vital national issues. In the late sixties population problems were coming to the forefront of our concerns. It seemed that in such fundamental activities as food production we had to keep running hard to stay in the same place. President Ferdinand Marcos, who was one of the signatories of the 1966 "Declaration on Population by World Leaders", then decided to formulate a population policy.

With the help of Dr. Mercedes Concepción, Dean of the Institute of Population Studies in the University of the Philippines, we called together a committee to discuss the problem and the probable courses of action. We reasoned that in such a predominantly Catholic country, a negative position from the Church would nullify any policy on population from the start. We, therefore, invited the Catholic hierarchy—this meant all the bishops of the dioceses throughout the country—to a meeting in the Palace. In the course of the discussions, I suggested that the Government would not issue any Executive Order on population unless the text was agreeable to them collectively. This was accepted and the bishops created a small committee to go over the language of the proposed Order.

It was only after they had agreed to the text that I forwarded the Order to the President for his consideration and final decision. The manner of preparing the Executive Order was the crucial step for the cooperation of the Church at that time in the Philippines Population Programme. A few years later, as head of UNFPA, one of the early projects I approved was the delivery of $40 thousand worth of thermometers for the Responsible Parenthood Council of the Philippines to support a pilot family planning project in which the Council was cooperating with the Department of Education and the Council of Bishops.

In UNFPA there has been no hindrance in assisting Catholic countries, Responsible Parenthood Councils, and other Catholic organizations. This is covered by the Fund's neutral policy of acting only in accordance with the policies and requests of governments. As a proof of the effectiveness of this approach there is now at least one Fund-assisted population programme in each of the Catholic countries of the developing world. This includes the funding of seminars and research projects, census and other forms of data collection, demographic studies, grants for equipment and assistance to maternal and child health service programmes, and the "planification familiar" in Latin America. In addition we have allocated almost $600,000 to Catholic organizations which have wanted to do various kinds of educational work.

The scope of this effort was the subject of my conversations with Pope Paul VI when I had an audience with him during World Population Year. I recalled in his previous statement delivered by Monsignor G. Benelli, that he had shown acute concern for the population problems when he said: "We are aware that the growing number of people, in the world taken as a whole and in certain countries in particular, presents a challenge to the human community and to governments. The problems of hunger, health, education, housing and employment become more difficult to solve when the population increases more rapidly than the available resources."

As we spoke in this interview I indicated the need for furthering the consciousness of people on the population problem and the collaboration between the United Nations effort and the Church. The Pope, in turn, emphasized his views within the two encyclicals and made certain that I did not lose track of them—by giving me beautifully bound copies of each. And, as I prepared to leave his study, he said: "I give my blessing to you, your wife, your son—and your future children."

A Matter of Values

I have always believed that working in such a sensitive area as population where every project touches the most elusive part of man's life—the act of procreation—it would be extremely shortsighted if we did not, while working on these worldly matters, think seriously of the ultimate reason why we undertook this task in the first place.

Every human act to which we attribute an apparent reason is in reality a refraction of what each human being deeply believes to be important for himself. All our lives our manifest behavior is directed by a hierarchy of these beliefs. These determine our values—and as we cannot escape having values it is better for the sake of clarity to state them explicitly.

If I were to be asked why I consider working in UNFPA such an important task, I would without hesitation say: "I believe that I am working sincerely for the preservation of the human species on this planet." I feel very few can disagree with me on this very general proposition. It answers: "Why?" It is in the "how" afterwards, that I feel committed to explain myself. Let me attempt to do so.

In the millennia that man has existed on this planet, the one sure way to survive natural calamities, diseases, and accidents has been to reproduce in large numbers. This biological necessity has been institutionalized in man's religions, mores, and habits. However, as man grew in knowledge and acquired better control of his environment through science, his ability to reproduce in large numbers and to prolong his life also increased. This posed a new and threatening problem—large numbers require equally large resources. The rapid growth of population is now depleting the resources that support life.

Man's biological urge to reproduce, which in the past was encouraged, has now to be rationally restrained. The ideal must now be to achieve the right number within the limits of existent resources to allow each human being to develop to full maturity. The message is not the diminution of numbers but the attainment of balance.

This is the global rationale for all population programmes, whether they are for the present designed for the decrease or increase of population in particular countries. Thus far, the mathematical projections supporting this view have not been successfully repudiated by those who think otherwise, and it is for this reason that I feel justified in continuing with our work.

If we look at the present relationships between countries, there is even more reason why we should continue with our efforts. There are today massive disparities in the quantity and value of resources available in different parts of the world. We can no longer assume with optimism as we did years ago that an equitable distribution of resources can be accomplished by sheer engineering. Better knowledge of their availability and the rate of their depletion have changed our thinking. We now know that there must be a curb on the production and consumption of raw materials and more attention paid to their judicious use.

The more affluent must learn to limit their wants. How is this to be done? I believe by a restored recognition of the finite. Countries consuming the lion's share of resources seem to have lost sight of the goal that impelled them to accumulate in the first place. There is a growing sense in these countries that something is missing from a life that has lost the deeper satisfactions arising from a fundamentally sound relationship with the rest of nature. It is time to put a recognition of limitation at the forefront of our consciousness.

So far, international assistance in techniques and resources has been largely one way, from the developed to the developing countries. What can the developing countries offer the rest of the world? People who live under conditions of scarcity in poorer but less-spoiled environments are ever conscious of one important norm—they have to limit their wants. It is in this that they are rich—and a sense of this together with a deeper empathy, is what they can give in return to the developed world.

It is with this understanding that I look upon the work of the Fund in giving population assistance as an effort at reciprocity and a restoration of the sense of balance.

CHAPTER 8

The Road through Bucharest

In 1970 the General Assembly of the United Nations on the recommendations of the Economic and Social Council designated 1974 as World Population Year. It also called for an intergovernmental World Population Conference to be held during the year.[1]

There have been many doubts cast on the efficacy of "Years". One of the most frequent wisecracks is that you hold one year devoted to a special subject so that you can forget all about it for the next ten.

From the point of view of the Fund and our interest in advancing knowledge and understanding of population, the World Population Year (WPY) could not have been more timely. We were trying our hardest to get governments to give serious consideration to population matters irrespective of how they decided to tackle the situation afterwards. We had no doubts that once they recognized the influence of population matters on every aspect of national life that they would certainly act and not sink back into ten subsequent years of apathy.

We also welcomed the proposal for a World Population Conference to be the highlight of the Year in that it would bring together policymaking and other government officials, population experts, and representatives of aid programmes from all the member states of the United Nations to discuss population problems.

While grateful for the opportunities offered by the Year for stimulating awareness campaigns at both national and international levels, I realized that this meant that in 1974 a portion of our resources would have to be pulled away from supporting field work in order to carry out an effective worldwide information campaign.

[1] General Assembly Resolution 2683 (XXV) (11 December 1970). ECOSOC Resolutions 1484 (XLVIII) and 1485 (XLVIII) (3 April 1970).

But somehow or other we managed to hold the line in keeping up the level of population field work and at the same time launching an intensive informational and educational programme for the Year. One measure of the success of World Population Year was that 137 states and some 300 organizations sent representatives to the global conference and its related non-governmental Tribune and Youth Conference. Not to mention the fact that after three weeks of debate, struggle, confrontations, and curious alliances, a consensus was reached by nations and a World Plan of Action endorsed which is now providing guidelines for future planning.

How that all came about is the subject of this chapter.

The allocation of responsibility for WPY was laid down by ECOSOC in June of 1972[2] in a resolution requesting the Secretary-General "with the financial assistance of the United Nations Fund for Population Activities":

"(a) To announce the World Population Year and World Population Conference at an early date. . . .

"(b) To appoint, within the Department of Economic and Social Affairs and at the Assistant Secretary-General level, a Secretary-General for the World Population Conference . . . equipped with the necessary secretariat resources. . . .

"(c) To designate the Executive Director of the United Nations Fund for Population Activities as having responsibility for preparations for the World Population Year and to request him to take the necessary steps, having regard to the resources available, to establish a secretariat from within the Fund and to work closely with the Population Division, the Centre for Economic and Social Information, the Specialized Agencies and the relevant non-governmental organizations."

The resolution also urged the Secretary-General of the Conference and the Executive Director of the Fund "to cooperate to the extent necessary to ensure that preparations for the World Population Conference and the World Population Year proceed smoothly, bearing in mind the complementary nature of the activities of the Year and of the Conference".

This was a curious division of labour: the United Nations in designating

---

[2] ECOSOC Resolution 1672 (LIV) (2 June 1972).

previous "Years" and their accompanying conferences had entrusted the management of both events to one specific body. Normally this was a special secretariat. But in 1972 the Fund already had worldwide visibility, and many participants in the preparatory committees thought it should be given a more definitive part in the celebration. Stanley Johnson, the IPPF representative, persuaded his Government's representative to propose an active role for UNFPA. What came out in the final ECOSOC resolution was an ingenious device of not giving the total responsibility either to the Fund or the Population Division. The responsibility for the WPY was given to the Executive Director of UNFPA and the responsibility for the Conference to a Secretary-General staffed by the Population Division. A very unusual arrangement somehow obscured by the agreement that the World Population Conference was to be the highlight of the Year.

World Population Year

I was glad to be made responsible for WPY activities. Whatever these would turn out to be, I was sure they would lead to many new programming commitments in needy countries, and I was anxious that these should be related as closely as possible to other population programmes in progress in those countries.

I foresaw no difficulty in discharging our commitments in connection with the World Population Conference. In any case, the Secretary-General's designation of Antonio Carrillo-Flores, formerly both the Finance Minister and Foreign Minister of Mexico, as Secretary-General of the Conference, made our job in this regard easier and more enjoyable than I had anticipated.

The objectives of the Year also presented no difficulties for the Fund. They were to:

(a) Improve knowledge of and information on the facts concerning population trends and prospects, and the relevant associated factors.

(b) Sharpen awareness and heighten appreciation of population problems and their implications by individual governments, non-governmental organizations, scientific institutions, and the media.

(c) Provide effective education on population, family life, and reproductive functions through formal and other educational systems.

(d) Stimulate discussion and thinking on alternative policies, promotion of demographic considerations in development planning, and development of policies and programmes in the population field which individual governments might wish to undertake.

(e) Expand international cooperation in population fields and supply increased and suitable technical assistance to countries deserving it, and in accordance with their needs.

Of these we were already working vigorously on (a), (c), and (e) and to a lesser extent on (b) and (d). What was called for related primarily to the heightening of interest and the improvement of understanding of population matters around the globe.

To launch the WPY campaign I expanded and transformed our Public Information Section into the WPY Secretariat. Tarzie Vittachi, an Asian journalist and recipient of a Ramon Magsaysay Award for Journalism and Literature, was appointed Executive Secretary of the unit with a mandate to do everything possible to get the involvement of governmental ministries, national groups, non-governmental organizations, business, social and youth clubs, churches of all creeds, universities, and schools. He was assisted by Jyoti Singh, former Secretary-General of the World Assembly of Youth, who took charge of non-governmental participation. Virtually no outlet that would bring the Fund in touch with decision makers, or the people who would be affected by the decisions, was barred. In the end the WPY programme was certainly a strange mixture of information and substantive projects, but there were few sectors in both the developed and the developing world which did not know about the population effort.

Preliminary proposals for an information programme for the Year had been drawn up under the direction of Snowden Herrick of the United Nations Centre for Economic and Social Information (CESI). These suggestions proved very helpful to Vittachi and his group after the Fund was charged with responsibility for the Year. The new programme devised by Vittachi in collaboration with a great many organizations was heavily motivational in content, and laid considerable emphasis on public information activities. It also left room for the expansion and adaption of suitable components in substantive population programmes so that targets could be set for WPY achievements. Consequently, there was a notable acceleration in the implementation of many ongoing field programmes and of analytical studies of population situations.

The impact of the Year on the population programmes of the various agencies was no less impressive. With generous financial injections from the Fund to strengthen their capacity, the United Nations and other international organizations proceeded to initiate programmes of their own to demonstrate the influence of population on agriculture, industry, health, education, employment, economic advancement, and social welfare.

As 1974 drew closer and the public information programme began to take effect, the Fund was dealing with hundreds of national organizations and community groups all of which wanted to play their part in their own special spheres in forwarding the objectives of the Year.

Governments, too, showed remarkable celerity in entering into the spirit of the Year and requested assistance over and above the aid being given to other population programmes in order to engage in special campaigns and to establish interconnections between aspects of their regular programmes and the new undertakings. I must emphasize at this point that in the view of the Fund every year is WPY and we endeavoured to encourage programmes for 1974 which would provide the basis for or lead to long-term population work.

Moreover, both the Secretary-General of the Conference and I spent a lot of time encouraging governments to set up national population commissions which would pull all the population activities in their countries together under one umbrella and also provide a forum for the people working in them. In response, sixty-four nations set up such commissions, which was four times as many as for any previous United Nations Year.

Substantive Role of the News Media

In these efforts, UNFPA went way beyond the normal confines of such activities in the United Nations system. One of Vittachi's first moves was to establish a network of news gathering and news dissemination centres in different parts of the world. An important organization in this network, the Press Foundation of Asia, was already in existence and being assisted by the Fund to provide information services and facilities for journalists on development subjects. With the cooperation of its chief executive, Amitabha Chowdhury, its role was expanded to enlist the support of journalists and editors in the region in spreading the message of WPY. Based on this model the Fund assisted in setting up the Latin American Association of Development Journalists (ALACODE), to serve Latin America. This centre went into operation under the direction of Javier Ayala and Gabriel Ortiz. Shortly thereafter, the Regional Arab Centre for Information Studies in Population, Development and Reconstruction, was created in the Middle East. Headed by Abdul Monim El Sawy and Zubeir Seif Al Islam, this Centre has sought to stimulate interest among Arabic-speaking communities.

I also sought every opportunity of talking to the press. Speaking to a seminar of newsmen in Bogota in August 1973 I said that to make the public understand population problems, in all their variety and complexity, required their own keen and knowledgeable appreciation of the true significance and dimensions of the question. I said it was no longer possible for the media in the developing world to stand aloof from population problems, no longer sufficient for communicators to react to events that have already taken place and neglect the task of reporting where the past was taking us.

I knew from previous work in the Philippines that the government must know what is happening in the streets and villages if it is to function well and meet the needs of the people. Such two-way communication cannot exist without a well-informed and expert corps of journalists. I remembered a description of the journalist's work: "A good journalist takes a dull or specialist or esoteric situation and makes newspaper readers want to know about it. By doing so he both sells newspapers and educates people."

In our WPY activities we were trying to draw the press and other media into doing this to an increasing extent on population topics. In the effort we literally sprayed the world with initiatives: symposia, conferences, seminars, speeches, articles, books, and films. To help keep everyone informed we published monthly the *World Population Year Bulletin.* An information dossier containing feature items, photographs, and other graphic material was regularly distributed also to 1500 newspapers and press agencies.

Some of these publications were conventional, some less so. In the latter connection I might mention the books *A Matter of People* and *Voices for Life*, both put out by Praeger in collaboration with us. The first is a well-written account by Dom Moraes, the Indian poet, of his firsthand reactions to population problems and people concerned with them in a number of places in Asia, Africa, and Latin America. The second, which is subtitled *Reflections on the Human Condition*, is a remarkable collection of articles by a number of the most thoughtful people in the world on the broader setting of population problems.

The World Population Conference

The Fund, in addition to its own commitments in connection with WPY, had another important function, which was to give financial support for the Conference itself and related activities. In the end this sum reached $1.9 million, which was some 50 per cent of the total cost. The balance was provided by the United Nations from its regular budget.

The Conference called for most detailed planning, as it differed greatly from the two previous population conferences at which experts spoke in their own right. For the first time in population history it was a conference of governments, and the climate for the discussions as well as the locale had to be given close attention. Accordingly, the United Nations Population Commission was given the responsibility of acting as the formal preparatory committee.

It was obvious that government representatives would arrive at the Conference with statements in hand on their national situation, policies, and views. While this would be a vital element in the discussions, it was also necessary that they should have reached some understanding on population matters with their neighbours in their respective regions, and have given consideration to their individual roles in regard to an international effort.

To facilitate interchanges of this kind, the United Nations Secretariat with financing from the Fund held regional consultations with the governments in the five major regions and also set up four symposia dealing with important aspects of population. The symposia attracted much local and international notice. They were held in key cities and covered the following subjects: Population and Development—Cairo; Population and the Family—Honolulu; Population, Resources, and Environment—Stockholm; and Population and Human Rights— Amsterdam.

In the meantime, the United Nations Secretariat started work on a draft "World Population Plan of Action" under the direction of the Population Division's Leon Tabah and Riad Tabbarah. They took account of the results of the above meetings, the deliberations of an Advisory Committee of Experts and the Population Commission, and the various individual talks the Secretary-General of the Conference had had with government leaders. The United Nations organizations and the Fund also made contributions. Later this draft served as the main working paper for the Conference.

The Conference was scheduled for August 1974 in Bucharest, Romania. A great deal had been accomplished already in the preparatory stages and there was every possibility that delegates would come to Bucharest with knowledge, expertise, and national backing. But not only population factors were involved. Issues other than population had come into the picture. By the date of the Conference it was clear that discord between industrialized and less-industrialized countries over economic matters had dramatically increased.

Although Gross National Product growth rates in the less-industrialized countries had for the most part been high, they were much less impressive on a *per capita* basis owing to high rates of population growth. The gap in standards of living between industrialized and less-industrialized countries continued to grow. This caused distress, but few yet focussed on what resource experts and environmentalists were saying: that at present levels of technology and present rates of resource consumption there eventually would not be enough to go around.

This set of considerations and the idea of a different and more forceful way of dealing with problems burst upon the developing world like a blinding light when in 1973 in the aftermath of the Arab-Israeli war the Arab countries imposed an oil embargo on Europe, Japan, and the United States. For the first time many people began to ponder the meaning of a finite environment.

In the spring of 1974 the developing countries, led by Algeria, succeeded in convening a special session of the United Nations General Assembly, the outcome of which was a "Declaration on the Establishment of a New International Economic Order". It called for common interest and cooperation among all states, irrespective of their economic and social systems, to "correct inequalities and redress existing injustices, make it possible to eliminate the widening gap between the developed and developing countries, ensure steadily accelerating economic and social development and peace and justice for present and future generations . . .".

In the resolution the developing countries were saying that the solution of all other problems had to go forward together with the solution to inequities between developing and developed countries. Somewhere in the middle of this was population and I wondered if it could be made a common cause despite the widening rift.

The Conference was welcomed by Nicolae Ceausescu, President of the Socialist Republic of Romania, who emphasized the importance of the world gathering. Kurt Waldheim, Secretary-General of the United Nations, followed and said:

"All our most important problems are interrelated, affecting each other in complex ways: In this sense, what we face from both a national and international perspective, is one overriding problem, born out of the rapid pace of technological and political change, demanding innovative answers to the critical question: How can we improve the quality of life? One problem it may be, yet it reveals itself in distinct facets, each of which provides access to an ultimate solution and one of these is population change."

When the time came for me to speak I took the opportunity to air a matter that had been uppermost in my mind for a long time—the need for a society of sufficiency to replace the distortions of both excess and deprivation.

I explained that when we speak of a society of sufficiency for all we are not just speaking of the developing countries. Sufficiency for all, in this sense of an absence of excess as well as an absence of deprivation, is a concept which is valid internationally as well as nationally.

The pursuit of increasing wealth has meant greater and greater production, consumption, and waste, with consequently increasing damage to the ecological balance. Pollution does not respect national boundaries. Everyone, including the developing countries, is affected by the results of overloading the air and sea with waste products. Everyone, especially the developing countries, is affected by excess demand and the consequence of this demand on the supply of basic commodities which should by right be available at a fair and reasonable price to all.

Thus far the concept of progress has been largely appreciated in economic terms, and the pursuit of wealth has set ever higher standards of affluence at which to aim. Is it possible now, I asked, to limit our material demands? Can our priorities be changed so as to answer the needs of all?

For the sufficiency society of the future some values of both past and present may still be valid; but not values that spawn unbridled acquisitiveness. Rather, I urged, let us seek the values of cooperation and concern, of involvement in the lives of others, values which come from recognition that the lives and the fate of all are inextricably bound up with each other, that man is now interdependent between continents, as he once was within the confines of the village. Fortunately these values still exist in many parts of our world and must play a vital role in the future.

I noted that there were signs that a change in positions and in attitudes had already begun. Growing national pride and self-confidence in many countries were bringing about a re-evaluation of national needs and wants which was both more in line with the realities of existing social structures and better adapted to the dictates of change. There was more willingness among national leaders to institute and accept change and to root out those aspects of the social and economic system which were obstacles to development.

Among industrialized countries there was a new willingness to participate in the evolution of new approaches. There was a growing acceptance that the values of growth and acquisition were not the most appropriate for our times, in a world whose resources and capacity to absorb the effects of human activity were limited. In the transition from scarcity to sufficiency, technologies and techniques were emerging—some new, some adapted, but in either case appropriate to the needs and values of development.

I emphasized that this is the context in which the problems of population must be seen. The adoption of sensible and enlightened policies in this field is an essential step for all countries, whether developed or developing, on their road towards becoming sufficiency societies in the sense that I have used that term.

Toward the end of my address, however, I had to return to what had become a recurring theme—money. By this time it had become very apparent that there was going to be a vast upsurge of requests for assistance, requests we had invited and now had to meet. I estimated, somewhat to the surprise of the delegates, that about US$500 million would be needed for the period 1974-7 to respond to the most urgent requirements of the developing countries for the Fund's support. Of course this rapid expansion of demand on the Fund, while presenting a financial challenge, was also satisfying in that it testified to the viability of the multilateral approach in this most sensitive of all matters and to the acceptability of the Fund's own procedures. A momentum had been generated and an atmosphere had been created in which it was possible to think in terms of solutions to problems which at one time seemed insoluble. I asked, "Will that momentum and that atmosphere be maintained?"

The answer to this question, it seemed to me, would depend greatly on governmental commitments to the World Population Plan of Action. After all in order to give the Plan substance, it would be necessary for countries and communities to design and put into effect their own national plans of action in accordance with their own special conditions and with their own resources. I assured the delegates that whatever the outcome of their discussions and whatever the form of the Plan that was agreed upon, UNFPA, with the cooperation of the United Nations system and other inter-governmental and non-governmental bodies, was ready to offer every possible assistance to enable countries to implement their decisions.

Then the Conference settled down to work. The draft World Population Plan of Action served as the primary working paper. Because population problems are inescapably complex and far-reaching in their interrelations with almost all other aspects of human life, and because feelings of the developing countries on many economic and social issues were now running very high, the draft was a very broad document. Nevertheless, it had a stormy passage.

It stated eight principles, for the most part drawn from technical or moral standards already approved by the international community. They embraced the principles on which the Fund had been working from the beginning. The six objectives stated by the Plan constituted a succinct summary of the purposes we had been pursuing in our programming, although going somewhat beyond them with respect to mortality and migration.

The draft Plan did not fix quantitative objectives for birth rates but did suggest targets for the further reduction of death rates. Stating that the majority of the world population lives in countries which wish to reduce their fertility, the draft Plan recognized two types of measures for reducing family size: those which permit all couples to achieve the family size they desire, and those which influence this desire by changes in economic and social factors. The first, the draft included among international recommendations; the second, it left to the decision of governments, although it recommended some steps in the fields of marriage, the status of women, the status of children, and education.

All in all it was a very inclusive, well-balanced document but nonetheless, the debate at the Conference was intense and conflict-laden. This partly resulted from the broader issues of equity and justice which had characterized the Sixth Special Session of the General Assembly. There was also a series of acrimonious exchanges on the proper weight to be assigned to the influence of rapid population growth on economic change and how it should be dealt with. Significantly, however, despite a very large number of amendments to the draft, at one point over 300, the World Plan of Action was eventually approved with hardly a dissenting voice and included all the essential features of the draft.

One of the key aspects of the draft Plan had been carried over from the 1968 International Conference on Human Rights in Teheran. It now became an integral part of a political consensus involving 136 countries. "All couples and individuals have the basic right to decide freely and responsibly the number and spacing of their children and to have the information, education and means to do so; the responsibility of couples and individuals in the exercise of this right takes into account the needs of their living and future children, and their responsibilities toward the community." Here was the basis for governmental programmes the world around.

In addition to outlining suggested or recommended courses of action covering all the fields in which UNFPA had been already responding to government requests for assistance, the Plan called, "in view of the magnitude of the problems and the consequent national requirements for funds", for "considerable expansion of international assistance in the population field . . .". The General Assembly of the United Nations added weight to this appeal at its next regular session following the Conference. We were glad of this.

The acrimony of the debate was widely reported in the press and tended to obscure from some newspaper readers the significance of the fact that when all the arguments and counter arguments on population and other matters were done, the world community had committed itself to a highly important policy document.

The next major event in the eventful year, 1974, was the World Food Conference which was held in Rome in November. This gave me an opportunity to recommend that "in considering the immediate steps to be taken in the solution of the food crisis, governments should not lose sight of the long-run effect of population growth which will determine basically the nature, scope and intensity of the future food problem".

I think it is of great significance that the delegates, who came to Rome to consider food, passed a resolution which called for "achievement of a desirable balance between population and food supply", endorsed the World Population Plan of Action and specifically noted that unprecedented population growth "had doubled the world's population in a single generation".

Despite discord on other subjects, the world at last recognized that population growth affected not one but all nations, and not one but all nations must help deal with the consequences.

CHAPTER 9

Taking Stock

Bucharest sent everyone home with something to think about. The governments which had endorsed the World Population Plan of Action had virtually made a promise to engage in sustained, watchful population work. The Fund had unconditionally been given the responsibility of helping them to do so. The United Nations system had received a strong vote of confidence for its involvement in the population field.

I myself felt that the Fund had come of age in that, appearing for the first time before a critical world forum, it had been recognized as one of the main channels of international population assistance. What is more, the delegates at the Conference had urged that its capacity for aid-giving should be strengthened.

In retrospect I realized the wisdom of the separation of the Year from the Conference. It kept the Fund away from the lines of controversy on substantive issues and, as the Conference proceeded, the Fund's operational programmes became a significant factor in maintaining the stability of the discussions. Even when dissent was at its peak they provided the soothing evidence of successful population work being carried out by over a hundred countries.

For the moment I was satisfied. The Fund had ridden through unharmed, and come out stronger, from a conflict which had involved the passionate participation of the very articulate spokesmen of African, Arab, Latin American and Asian countries as well as militant groups representing different ideological views.

But, like an athlete flexing his muscles before a big race, at the beginning of 1975 the time had certainly arrived to take stock of the Fund's assets and capabilities before moving too precipitately into the new phase which was opening up before us. Perhaps because I had expended so much thought and energy in finding and compensating for what I considered weaknesses in the Fund's programme, I was quite impressed at the many sound alliances and operational partnerships the Fund had been able to establish in little more than five years.

As the Conference recognized, the Fund had helped to build up an effective international population assistance programme within the United Nations system. Without the cooperation of the agencies or governments and of other private organizations this could never have been achieved. But that cooperation had to be won.

At this point I should like to acknowledge the help that Rudolph Peterson, Hoffman's successor as Administrator of UNDP, gave the Fund during his four-year incumbency. His policy of delegating responsibility and at the same time providing helpful counsel enabled the Fund to have the continued flexibility and autonomy it needed during this period.

In all its actions UNFPA had tried to be open in its operations and intentions, willing to listen to the opinions of others, and responsive to their needs and wishes. To use current jargon, we kept our feedback loops open and adapted to our environment on the basis of the information received. Our openness certainly made criticism of us more likely and more frequent. At the same time it made it possible for us to deal with misunderstandings expeditiously and effectively.

This approach also had its effect on the organizations in the United Nations system. It was no secret that in the late 1960s inter-agency meetings on the subject of population were frequently very controversial and usually disappointingly indecisive. The Fund, however, proved to be the binding element, and by a process of inducement and cooperation succeeded in involving the United Nations organizations in joint programmes and in utilizing their staff and their specialized competencies for population undertakings. Disagreements between the Fund and agencies now seldom arise. When they do they are usually concerned with the priorities for the allocation of scarce resources, always a legitimate subject for argument.

The uses of UNFPA's resources were potentially a matter of disagreement also among the countries participating in the Fund. Most of the major donors had considerable experience in population work through their own bilateral programmes and consequently came into the multilateral sphere with set ideas on how the whole business should be handled. The minor donors, on the other hand, while less specific in their attitudes, still wanted to have a substantial say in the kinds of projects that were assisted.

It is greatly to their credit that after a series of discussions with the Fund both parties were willing to modify their positions and support programmes that bore the stamp of the United Nations system. Fund-sponsored discussions between the donor governments and the recipient countries also played a large part in promoting understanding of the Fund's policies of neutrality and responsiveness which, as I have already pointed out, placed the onus for programme development squarely on the shoulders of the officials of the developing countries themselves.

One of the Fund's most useful functions was to act as a buffer between recipients and donors so that donors could make contributions to the Fund in line with their motives, and recipients could receive assistance they had requested in line with theirs, without worrying about the intentions of the others.

In these ways, conflict—which could have paralysed the Fund's work—was avoided and significant progress made towards helping nations to adopt a broad international view of population policies.

A notable example of a move towards more liberal positions was the change in attitude of the French Government in regard to the problems which high rates of population growth, not a serious problem in France, might pose for other countries. The adjustment in French opinion towards support of population activities was important to the Francophone countries of Africa and opened the way to an examination of demographic conditions and population problems by governments previously disinterested in such investigations.

The Fund has also succeeded in lessening the differences on population issues among countries in the developing world. The reason for this success was that the Fund could accommodate all views through its ability to support a wide range of projects, and through its policy of non-intervention except on points of technical feasibility and suitability for Fund financing.

On assuming the role of leader in the population field, as instructed by the General Assembly and ECOSOC, the Fund had a commitment to increase coordination among other international and national population programmes. We sought to do this by co-opting some organizations as executing partners in Fund projects, in other instances by providing them with financing for projects of mutual interest, and in others, by organizing meetings and seminars which would activate exchanges of information and expertise between international, national, and private organizations. By thus encouraging involvement and stimulating interaction, the Fund helped to build communication networks encompassing both substantive and promotional activities which greatly strengthened the overall national programmes.

In particular, the Fund's support of non-governmental organizations on an unprecedented scale for the United Nations system brought together many previously unrelated groups and led to permanent working relationships which immeasurably increased their collective capacities. These organizations had frequently pioneered population work in countries in which the government was not quite ready to formulate a national population policy. Until World Population Year came along, however, they were seldom linked with other international and bilateral efforts in the same field. In all the Fund has assisted the programmes of fifty-six of these organizations.

To estimate the outcome of an awareness campaign of the kind the Fund engaged in, especially during World Population Year, is usually difficult if not impossible. But the combination of intensified information work and short-term population activities directed towards generating long-term programmes, had clearly identifiable results. Population policies and programmes, including the controversial subject of family planning, became respectable and acceptable, both as international concepts and as national undertakings. Countries came to accept the validity of measures they saw other governments adopt of their own free will.

The cumulative effect of this focus on population matters can be seen not only in the number of countries that have adopted national population policies and programmes within the last six years but also in the delegations which cast supportive votes on population items at international conferences—witness the consensus reached at Bucharest.

Programme Delivery

The Fund's stature and influence can best be assessed in the size and scope of its programme.

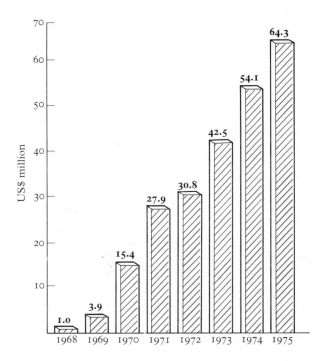

FIG. 2. Increase in contributions, 1969 to 1974 and estimated for 1975.

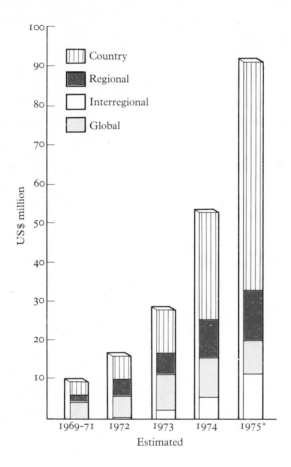

FIG. 3. Expenditure by regional coverage, 1969/71 to 1974 and estimates for 1975.

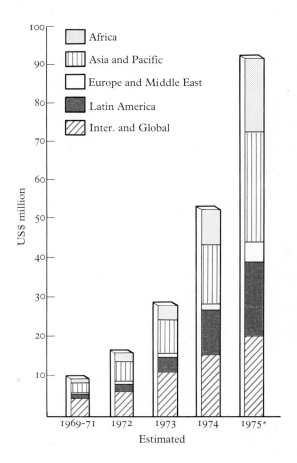

FIG. 4. Expenditure by geographic area, 1969/71 to 1974 and estimates for 1975.

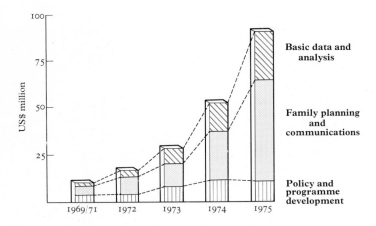

FIG. 5. Actual and planned expenditures by major population activities, 1969/71 to 1974 and estimated for 1975.

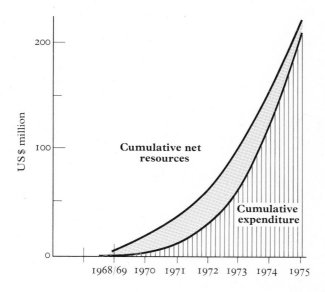

FIG. 6. UNFPA resources ever received and expenditure ever made at year's end, 1968/9 to 1974, and estimates for 1975.

By the end of 1975, cumulative resources had reached some $240 million. Figure 2 shows the increase in contributions by year. $200 million had been allocated for the support of 1382 projects benefiting 106 developing countries and areas. National projects, of which twenty-three were comprehensive country programmes, accounted for $107 million and regional and interregional undertakings for $93 million. Figure 3 shows the changes in this balance over the years.

Geographically, the Fund had spent over $60 million to assist countries in Asia and the Pacific area where the bulk of the world's people live. About $35 million each was spent in the African and the Latin American regions and some $8.6 million went to the Middle East. Figure 4 shows the regional expenditures by year.

Over half the Fund's available resources have been directed towards family planning and related communications projects. The next largest category, basic data collection and demographic analysis, has received close to 30 per cent. The remaining funds have been devoted to what we call policy and programme development. Figure 5 shows this distribution by year.

There was a considerable acceleration in the rate of implementation of the Fund's field programme in 1974 and 1975. By 1975 our implementation rate was well over 80 per cent of budgets approved for that year—a highly satisfactory level. Figure 6 illustrates the expenditure rate against resources on hand.

Various moves had contributed to this programming record. The issuance of clear guidelines to govern the form and content of project requests had helped to reduce false starts and to avoid revisions. The growing experience within the Fund on how and where to obtain the most appropriate technical expertise and on how to deal with the complexities of project preparation had helped to shorten the time required to organize the participation of organizations involved in the programmes. The greater familiarity of these agencies with the Fund's programme had also played an important part in improving coordination of effort.

The introduction of direct funding for government projects had resulted in new account being taken of the technical and substantive skills available in the recipient countries. In this way it was possible to reduce the number of international experts being recruited for projects—a major cause of delays in project operations. And, lastly, the presence of the

UNFPA Coordinators had cut to a minimum the difficulties and timelags inherent in long-range correspondence.

In addition, special measures designed to spur local initiative were introduced to facilitate project operations. Because of shortage of supplies the Fund moved to make commodity purchases locally as well as internationally. In this way delays were reduced, economies effected, and national suppliers given a share of the pie. Governments were helped to finance the basic costs of projects which were unlikely to show benefit returns for some time, and the Fund began providing local currency support for recurrent costs—an expense that the government is usually asked to carry and which has been the death of many a good enterprise. The start-up of undertakings such as the building of a condom factory was accelerated by a Fund decision to meet some capital costs on a grant basis and thus give a new stimulus to local industries.

This was not all a matter of statistics and bureaucracy. Local support on one occasion led us to add a team of donkeys—immediately called the "United Nations donkeys"—to the staff of one field office. The purpose was to provide transport for enumerators taking a census in less accessible outlying areas. Unfortunately three of the donkeys plunged from a cliffside and were killed. The census records went with them. The owner of the donkeys immediately claimed compensation. The Director of the Census Programme argued that the price paid for the use of the donkeys covered such risks. To settle the matter the owner arrived on the Director's doorstep with three sheep and slaughtered them before the eyes of the flabbergasted office staff. In this way, according to Bedouin custom, he had proved that in making such a sacrifice he had right on his side. The Director paid up—$300.

Perhaps the most important innovation in UNFPA programming has been to allow recipient governments to make their own choice of implementing agencies either national or international, or a combination of both, for certain programmes. Besides stimulating governments to take a continuing and sustained interest in the population projects they themselves have sponsored, this particular initiative has had the very salutary effect of involving more national organizations and qualified local personnel in Fund-supported projects.

This direct funding policy is illustrated in an Asian country programme where all the financing flows from UNFPA via the UNDP Resident

Representative to national agencies implementing the projects. These agencies carry the total responsibility for disbursing and accounting for UNFPA funds. Several international organizations selected by the Government provide technical assistance to the projects and share in monitoring them but do not perform any of their usual financial functions.

For the largest single project—the family planning programme of the Ministry of Health and Social Affairs—the Government has created an In-Country Technical Assistance Mission. Its task is to provide technical consultation and assistance to officials and technical people at all levels in the national family planning programme. It is made up of twenty-three national specialists drawn from such professional and scientific disciplines as reproductive medicine, demography, administration and management, research, and education and communication.

Another direct assistance agreement, contracted with India, is notable in that it is much the biggest the Fund has yet financed. In the summer of 1970, when I began the negotiations, the Indian Government was in the process of actively challenging the traditional practice by donors of assigning their own experts to all development assistance projects. In the population area they correctly claimed they had available sufficient expertise of their own and needed only outside funds for foreign exchange components and innovative programme activities. It was not very long before they asked us for a direct grant to support what at that time was a new programme activity—mass vasectomy camps.

It took almost eighteen months, but we finally were able to agree to the somewhat radical act of providing a large sum of money ($1 million) without attaching foreign experts to oversee its expenditure. Our grant caused some comment within the donor community but it was a very important precedent for us in that it facilitated the signing of several programme agreements with governments possessing expertise but insufficient funds to expand their population activities.

The outcome of this initial grant to India was a $40 million five-year comprehensive agreement which we signed in 1974. All but $1 million of this is to be given directly to the Government to help it expand its family planning services and to investigate new programme strategies.

In all, $7 million worth of projects were financed under direct funding arrangements in 1974 and over $12 million in 1975. Among the countries directly executing Fund-assisted projects in addition to India were Costa Rica, Egypt, Jamaica, Kenya, the Republic of Korea, Malaysia, Pakistan, the Philippines, Thailand, Tunisia, and Turkey.

Many of these programming innovations were not received with universal plaudits. So it was with considerable pleasure that I saw that UNDP had incorporated some of them in its paper on "New Dimensions for Technical Cooperation" prepared by I. G. Patel, Deputy Administrator. I was equally pleased to see that this paper was warmly endorsed by the UNDP Governing Council in June 1975.

Exciting as all these developments undoubtedly were, the Fund's basic reputation rested, and will continue to rest, on the effectiveness of its field programme.

Major Global Projects

In casting my mind back over the development of our programme I feel that the Fund's greatest achievement has been to maintain consistent support for the more usual kind of projects requested by governments, and at the same time to reserve enough money to help launch important programmes of common concern that could never have come into being without the seed money contributed by the Fund.

I was in part motivated by a feeling that if the Fund did not join in the search for wider knowledge and technical and scientific advancement in the population field, few government programmes could or would; and in part by a determination to prevent the Fund's programme from becoming stereotyped and, therefore, unreceptive to progressive ideas.

I acknowledged that the Fund's primary responsibility at the beginning of the programme was undoubtedly to meet requests for assistance in the collection and use of basic population data and for starting or expanding family planning programmes. The closely related population communications and education fields rated priority consideration. But despite the validity of these claims on resources, the Fund took a series of decisions which opened up new avenues of research, gave governments insights into the art of population, and sharpened the use of sophisticated tools for teaching and training.

One of the most important of these major programmes was the World Fertility Survey. This is the largest single social science research project ever undertaken. Jointly financed by UNFPA and USAID it is being executed by the International Statistical Institute, which draws on the services of the world's best-qualified statisticians and demographers. The purpose of the project is to provide reliable data on fertility patterns and levels as an aid to economic and social planning. Information on fertility differentials can only be obtained through special surveys. While a number of these surveys had been conducted in the past, their usefulness was limited due to inadequate control, shortcomings in tabulation and analysis, and lack of agreement on the concepts used. The project is aimed at establishing a methodology which will permit worldwide comparability of data from surveys taken in many countries.

A somewhat similar effort to help policymakers is concerned with a research and action programme on population and employment under the World Employment Programme, being undertaken by the ILO. The Programme seeks to increase understanding of the interrelations between employment growth and changes in population growth, structure, and location. Models are being constructed based on research by distinguished scholars which will demonstrate the interaction between levels of fertility, spatial distribution of population, and types of employment. By the end of 1975 these were already being used by the economic planners of Brazil, Kenya, the Philippines, and Yugoslavia.

Management of population programmes is the subject of still another fascinating project which brings together the heads of many of the leading population programmes in Africa, Asia, Latin America, and the Middle East to share thoughts and experience with leaders of management research and training organizations. The participants meet periodically as members of the International Committee on Management of Population Programmes (ICOMP). Aziz Bindary of Egypt is its dynamic Chairman. Suwardjono Surjaningrat of Indonesia, Wan Fook Kee of Singapore, Conrad Lorenzo of the Philippines, A. A. Armar of Ghana, and Victor Morgan of Costa Rica have served prominently from the programme side. Gerardo Cornejo, N. P. Sen, Henry Gomez, and Sagar Jain have made significant contributions from the academic side.

The spread of expertise in population programme administration has been greatly advanced by this group plus other senior government officials, Mezri Chkir of Tunisia and A. M. Sardari of Iran among them, on whom the success of national programmes rests.

There are, of course, many other undertakings of common concern requiring high professional specialization, such as the Law and Population Project under the supervision of Luke Lee of Tufts University in the United States. In this project, institutions in developing countries have been aided in making studies of laws and administrative practices related to population, and, in particular, to fertility. These studies have provided information of critical importance to lawmakers wishing to institute appropriate policies and programmes. No less important are the companion studies on cultural values and population policies being carried out in ten countries by local organizations working in collaboration with the American-based Institute of Society, Ethics, and Life Sciences.

Another area in which the Fund can claim a modicum of success is in opening up two-way channels between the national and international enterprises. This is best illustrated by training programmes. Virtually all UNFPA-supported programmes emphasize the importance of in-country training, drawing when necessary on regional services and facilities. This system has proved very effective in the use made of the regional demographic centres, which in addition to providing supplementary training facilities for countries in the region also concern themselves with other population activities. A case in point is the Latin American Demographic Centre (CELADE) which under the leadership of Carmen Miro, organizes teaching, advisory, and research activities in demography and population dynamics but which has also helped countries seeking its assistance to give attention to other aspects of population. Similarly, the Cairo Demographic Centre, directed by Soleiman Huzayyin, has been providing training for students mainly from the Arab and Moslem countries, while in the Sub-Sahara two demographic institutes, one English-speaking the other French, are providing technical and advisory services to countries in this sub-region and have also taken on the onerous task of training personnel needed for national demographic programmes and for the African census round.

The African Census Programme has combined international expertise with direct budgetary support to twenty-one African nations, fifteen of which have never before held an organized census. The total amount of assistance which covers the Fund's financial support, the technical assistance being provided by the United Nations, and the aid to the individual country programmes, has amounted to some $13 million. Under these allocations, expert assistance has been given to countries in planning and executing their censuses and for training technical and supervisory staff in methods and procedures by means of regional workshops and fellowships for training abroad. To ensure the provision of high calibre experts in the many specialized fields needed to complete the complex census operation, financing has also been furnished to expand the Statistical Division and Population Programme Centre of the Economic Commission for Africa and a block allocation made to the United Nations Department of Economic and Social Affairs in New York.

Projects such as these which demand an interplay between national and international know-how, which regard the regional elements as supplementary and contributory but not ruling factors in regard to country programmes, and which facilitate interchanges of experience between countries, to my mind, do more than political manoeuvres to promote international goodwill. They also provide the rationale for turning the spotlight, from time to time, away from the United Nations Security Council and on to the United Nations organizations which are devoting their energies to the less-glamorous but probably more important task of improving men's daily lot.

Fundraising: Second Stage

I am acutely aware that any goals the Fund has reached have been made possible by a sustained flow of contributions from seventy-seven countries of whom I am proud to say fifty-eight belong to the Third World. Without this assurance of financing, the Fund would have not been able to move forward so confidently and could easily have disappeared under a mound of mediocre projects of the "too little too late" variety.

In addition to my gratitude for the timely and consistent contributions, I am also very thankful that our donors agreed to establish the Fund as the single extra-budgetary funding source within the United Nations system for population programmes. The formerly diverse channels of donor support to various population activities have now been largely merged into one and directed to the Fund. I consider this a very tangible vote of confidence in the Fund's ability to identify and finance worthwhile population activities. This concentration of funding has been an important element in UNFPA's success in bringing some cohesiveness and coherence to population activities within the United Nations system.

It has been both a stimulus to launch vigorous field operations and an incentive to keep administrative costs low, that in a period of economic instability in the world the Fund's contributors have kept pace consistently with the needs of the growing programme. Since Denmark contributed the first $100,000 in 1967, UNFPA has received a cumulative total of nearly $240 million. More than 90 per cent of these funds have been contributed by nine major donors: Canada, Denmark, the Federal Republic of Germany, Japan, the Netherlands, Norway, Sweden, the United Kingdom, and the United States of America. Most of these have increased their contributions by substantial amounts each year. Pledges for 1975 were some 18.5 per cent higher than in the previous year.

This certainly represents loyal support from both developed and developing countries, the latter despite limited national budgets taking their share of responsibility.

We have managed to maintain the support of our traditional donors by keeping them fully informed about our operations—not just accomplishments but problems, deficiencies, and future trends. Their officers have been so well-informed about our work that talking to them' has been like having a discussion with a UNFPA officer. In this particular activity I was ably assisted by consultants like the late William Draper whom I have mentioned earlier, former US Senator Joseph Tydings, and our own fundraising officer, Audun Gythfeldt, a Norwegian from his country's development agency. We were also greatly helped by committed supporters in non-governmental organizations such as Larry Keegan, Phyllis Piotrow, and Robin Biddle Duke of the Population Crisis Committee, and Chojiro Kunii of the Japanese Organization for International Cooperation in Family Planning.

Because UNFPA does not have a regular pledging conference like that of UNDP and UNICEF, a feature common to most voluntary United Nations funds, I have also had to make periodic visits to the various heads of donor agencies responsible for deciding the annual contributions of governments to the Fund. These trips were not only necessary but extremely rewarding because I learned a lot from talking to these officials about their views on development assistance, a much-needed input into our own thinking in the Fund. This meant calling on these officials in their own countries or, when the work did not permit, conferring with them in

New York. Discussions were always brisk and businesslike but I think a new record was set when I visited Henry Kissinger, United States Secretary of State, to discuss the United States contribution to the Fund. Our meeting lasted exactly twenty minutes and when I left I had the assurance of an additional $2 million contribution—a decision-making formula I would like to see widely adopted.

This kind of support was a constant encouragement. But when taking stock one has to think in terms of debits as well as assets. By the middle of 1974 a wide programme of field activities was well under way but there was also a high increase in the volume of requests and the Fund began to foresee probable shortage of resources. We ourselves had invited this rapid expansion of demand and were morally obliged to meet it. If we could not, the loss of momentum would be very damaging. Experience has shown that owing to the relatively slow returns in population programmes, foreign assistance is needed as a stimulus at least in the early stages, and the programmes we were assisting had just got off the ground. The pressing question was how and where to raise more funds. I felt very strongly that if the Fund's very generous older donors were to be expected to give substantially more, I would have to show that there were newcomers who were willing to join the ranks.

Long before the Bucharest Conference I felt the need for reorienting our fundraising activities. Internally, I wanted to rely more on UNFPA officers to do fundraising and less on outside consultants, and, externally, to investigate the possibility of obtaining a share of the increased resources at the disposition of the oil-producing countries, an influential group of countries which had only minimally participated in the Fund's programmes.

I was fully aware of the endless stream of representatives of international and private development assistance organizations, religious organizations, women's groups, and youth groups, which were already knocking on the doors of the Arab decision makers. I also knew that had I been asking for food or some other form of direct subsistence within the concept of aid to the unfortunate called for by Muslim religious teaching, I would have got it. But assistance for population programmes was different. It had to be fully understood what this did and did not mean.

Under the circumstances I thought the thing to do when presenting the population case to the Arab leaders was to confine the discussions to those parts of our work which were of direct relevance to the Arab states. This began with the inaugural meeting of the Economic Commission for Western Asia (ECWA) early in 1974 where, through the help of its Executive Secretary, Mohamed Said Al-Attar, I had my first opportunity to appeal for an Arab contribution to UNFPA.

This presentation was followed by a subsequent meeting in Geneva of all Arab ambassadors called together by Charles Helou, former President of Lebanon, who had become interested in the Fund's activities. There I was given the chance to explain in more detail the operations of UNFPA in the Arab world, and the significance of a contribution through the United Nations to assist developing countries in their effort to solve the population problem. This explanation was well received. I followed this up with another meeting a few months later in Bucharest with all the Arab delegates to the World Population Conference. This included two ministers, Ali Al Ansari of Qatar and Mohamed Al Kindi of the United Arab Emirates. The subsequent Regional Consultation in Doha under the leadership of Al Ansari was another occasion I did not miss. With a large contingent of staff members, we detailed our work in the Arab countries and its contribution to their development efforts.

By this time, it must be noted, the Fund had been in operation for five years. Our projects in most of the Arab countries, particularly in census and demographic work, were beginning to show results. In the cases of the Yemen Arab Republic, the Peoples Democratic Republic of Yemen, Sudan, and Somalia, censuses had been completed with Fund assistance. Similarly, our large inputs in family planning programmes, particularly in Egypt and Tunisia, were gaining support from officials who believed that funding through UNFPA was an effective way of getting the required external assistance to their domestic efforts. The thought then came to me that rather than my explaining the Fund's objectives and programmes, would it not be more effective if the Arab ministers, who had seen the Fund perform in their countries, themselves testified as to its trustworthiness?

It was with this end in view and with the introduction given by Ismail Fahmy, Foreign Minister of Egypt, I approached Mahmoud Riad, Secretary-General of the Arab League and his deputy, Assad Al Assad, for a possible conference on population at a ministerial level, co-sponsored by both the Arab League and UNFPA. My proposal was accepted.

I then made a series of fast trips to the Arab world to encourage ministers to participate in the meeting. On several occasions I was honoured by audiences and meetings with Heads of State, such as His Majesty King Khaled Ibn Abdul Aziz of Saudi Arabia; President Habib Bourguiba of Tunisia; His Highness Shaikh Khalifa bin Hamad al-Thani, Emir of Qatar; and President Ibrahim Al-Hamdi of the Yemen Arab Republic. All of these Heads of State were not only warm and gracious hosts but also sincerely interested in population programmes and their relevance to their own countries and their region.

Time schedules in my fundraising trips were usually very tight. Unusually so in this particular case because I had a deadline to meet—attendance at the Arab League Meeting in May 1975 and at the Governing Council in June. I had therefore three weeks to visit eight countries. I made it as fast as we could by plane, car, and jeep. To keep on schedule, I even rode over deserts and mountains in a small single-engined plane where I was dumped in a tiny little seat together with all the luggage. It was uncomfortable all right, but I made the deadline.

There were always incidents on these trips to lighten things. On one occasion, because of the tonal similarity between *Iskan* and *Sukkan*— housing and population in Arabic, I was mistaken by the official I was calling on as the United Nations representative for housing projects. Here I was talking seriously about population with my host beaming and comprehending everything in housing terms. Either these terms are in fact indistinguishable or my gestures are more expressive than my discourse, but we ended the talk completely in agreement on all points.

At another time, including a nine-hour delay in between planes, it took me almost twenty-six hours to reach the Middle East from Latin America. Tired and on the verge of catching a cold, I was informed upon my arrival that the airline had lost my luggage. I refused to get upset and went straight to my hotel. But I had not even washed up when the telephone rang and I was told to be at the Palace within thirty minutes. I had been wearing my clothes for almost two days. Our Coordinator lent me his shirt but my crumpled suit was irreplaceable. Attired this way, I was taken with great ceremony to my audience with the Head of State. In this magnificent palace the conversation came out well and my host was apparently unconscious of my unconventional appearance. This must have been partly due to the good Arab practice of mixing cardamom with their coffee—it makes everything smell good.

The meeting of the Arab League took place on the 21st to 22nd of May 1975. One of the principal speakers was Sayed Marei of Egypt, who was the Secretary-General of the World Food Conference. Eleven ministers were present. The resolution that was adopted surpassed my most optimistic expectations. In one of its recommendations it urged member states to contribute no less than $25 million to UNFPA over a two-year period to finance assistance to population work in the Arab states.

We lost no time in securing the implementation of this resolution. In November 1975 I called a meeting of an advisory group to discuss the possibility of a mission to the Arab countries. Ali Al Ansari proposed and we accepted the plan to organize two missions to Arab League countries.

Under the able and skilful leadership of Al Ansari, the first mission from the Fund visited seven Arab countries in Africa in January. There was a very sincere understanding by the leaders of these countries of the needs of the Fund and their own population situations. The mission was able to secure the assurance of a $3.5 million contribution to the UNFPA for 1976 from Egypt, Somalia, Algeria, Morocco, Tunisia, Mauritania, and Libya, either in hard or local currencies. This was a major breakthrough.

Credit for the preparation, liaison work, and effective communications in my visits to the Arab countries and the Arab League meeting were due primarily to Faissal Cheikh el Ard, Soleiman Huzayyin, General Gamal Askar, Aziz Bindary, Hamid Fahmy, Abdul Latif Succar, Abdul Malek Farrash, Riad Tabbarah, and the Fund's Section Chief for our Middle East and North African projects. I was in fact the only non-Arab in this lively group of fundraisers.

Fundraising is the art of the possible. And the possibility that countries in a region would contribute to the Fund to meet the needs of that region encouraged me to look for similar leads in other parts of the world. In Latin America this took the form of visits to Heads of State. I began in 1974 with calls on President Pastrana Borrero of Colombia.

In 1975 I followed on with visits to President Echeverria of Mexico and President Carlos Andres Perez of Venezuela. In these latter meetings, it was unnecessary to explain the importance of population programmes as both Presidents were fully committed to programmes in this field. Mexico had already contributed to the Fund in local currency and was carrying out welfare programmes with family planning components. My appeal to

Venezuela to assist Latin American countries through UNFPA met with a positive response from the President.

In the same way as all the arrangements for the trips to the Arab countries had been made by Arabs, in this case all the arrangements were made by Latins. The people directly concerned were the Fund's Section Chief for Latin America, Miguel Albornoz, Luis Olivos and William Visser.

By utilizing UNFPA staff members who speak the language of the regions in this effort, I was not only facilitating communication with prospective donors but also training the officers to undertake these missions themselves without having to rely on fundraising consultants. I realize that this was in addition to their normal duties, but the Fund must have virtuosity if it is to survive in the rough and tumble of population work.

But fundraising in this traditional manner, we estimated, would not meet our needs for 1976 onwards. We had to explore other modalities for increasing our resources.

One such approach was to ask UNDP to investigate the possibility of population work, in projects closely integrated with development programmes, being financed under their Indicative Planning Figures (IPF). The IPF shows the amount of external aid which will be provided by UNDP over a five-year period to any one country in relation to its estimated national potentialities and needs. Several countries, in agreement with UNDP, have indicated that they wish to undertake part of their population programmes under such IPF funding, e.g. in connection with censuses. The extent of such collaboration, of course, is dependent on how much UNDP has already been committed under these IPF and thus on the resources still available.

Another approach, which will lead to additional financing for country programmes, involves collaboration between the Fund and bilateral aid programmes on particular projects. Here, UNFPA, with the approval of the potential recipient, obtains bilateral financing for projects which the Fund has fully screened and would support if the funds were available.

Surprisingly enough, the apparently prosaic process of fundraising calls for an enormous amount of imagination and inventiveness—in addition to a lot of time and hard work. I am fortunate in having around me so many people with these characteristics.

CHAPTER 10

At the Gateway

In the last six years, despite a new awareness and many action programmes, the world's population continues to grow rapidly. Although birth rates have begun to decline in a number of countries the present rate of decline is too slow to avoid intensification of a very wide range of problems of great importance for human welfare. Indeed, the momentum of population growth is such that, even taking account of these birth-rate declines, world population may well grow to three or even four times its present size before it levels off. Meanwhile, in a related process, cities are growing at an even more rapid rate and one which involves great strains on economic and political systems.

In these six years, moreover, the world has become aware that the resources available to support the growing numbers of people are finite. We are entering a period of progressive relative scarcity at least until the development of energy from other than traditional sources. As well as threatening hardship, this fact, coupled with modern communications and the growth in the explosiveness and numbers of weapons, contains potentialities of conflict.

However, I have been very much encouraged to see, as was particularly evident at the Seventh Special Session of the General Assembly in September 1975, that as well as a general awareness of the reasons for conflict, there is also a general awareness of the importance of finding ways in which disputes can be adjudicated peacefully.

Population has been an important factor in the genesis of the problems underlying these disputes. It must be an important factor in their solution. While much growth is inevitable what happens will depend ultimately on what we do.

The Changing Scene

On the population question there are now three dominant and contending schools of thought. The first, alarmed by demographic trends and impatient with the slow reaction from governments, advocates strong, radical measures such as "triage" and compulsory measures. Fortunately, there are no proponents so far of this view within the United Nations legislative bodies. In the main the other two schools dominate discussion on population. One believes that family planning within maternal and child health services is essential if high fertility rates are to be reduced. The other maintains that development programmes by themselves with their consequent effects on the economic and political structures of countries will "take care" of the population problem. The Bucharest Conference sought to reconcile these two viewpoints by conceptualizing population within a general development strategy.

The final consensus of the Conference, however, did not resolve the issues with sufficient precision to serve as a tactical blueprint for action. Some light is shed on this by recent history.

In the First Development Decade, economic planners were more or less certain of their strategy that self-sustaining growth could be induced by a proper mix of investments in the various economic sectors. It was believed that if the right techniques were applied and the economy reacted properly, the increase in the Gross National Product would indicate this growth. The approach was easily quantifiable and could be programmed readily. A similar approach was made with population programmes in their early phases, particularly because of their heavy emphasis on family planning. To control fertility rates, couples were encouraged to use contraceptives. The success of the programme could be measured by a periodic count of acceptors. Both these approaches had the virtues of clarity of objectives, programmability, and measurability of results.

The Second Development Decade and the Bucharest Conference changed the thinking on these subjects. Development is no longer viewed simply in terms of economic indicators. Its goals are no longer as precise. Employment, redistribution of income, rural development, and the improvement in the quality of life are some of the objectives that have been stressed by development planners. Similarly, the Bucharest Conference radically broadened population concepts. Family planning or demographic work are no longer sufficient. With the insistence on the interconnection between population and development, programmes relying primarily on family planning are seen as too narrow. But what is the substitute for family planning and how does it fit into development?

No answer can be immediately forthcoming although a trend seems to be developing towards greater caution in adopting the policies and models of the developed countries and more vigorous reliance on the developing countries' own capacities to conceptualize and direct their efforts. The human element is becoming more dominant in technology. In population planning this has become identical with the view that programmes are formulated not just to deal with numbers but to improve the lives of people.

Our experience has convinced us that this humanizing trend in development can be achieved by giving countries the opportunity to decide for themselves what they want with their development and population programmes. By enlarging the degree of participation in making decisions, implementation—whether it is within a small organization or a national bureaucracy—is facilitated.

As I have described earlier, with this approach we have succeeded in awakening the consciousness of governments and non-governmental organizations to population problems and have stimulated programmes for their solution. But the work done thus far is but an initial phase beginning a much more urgent and compelling exercise to reach the individuals who, after all, make the decisions on the size of their own families. Governments are only motivators and providers, they do not make the ultimate decision. There is, therefore, a need to widen and deepen the understanding of people so that they are willing and able to consider their decisions on population matters including family size in the same way as they reach conclusions on food and the other imperatives of life. In this second phase no effort and no resources, both national and international, must be spared to secure their commitment.

Rhetoric and Understanding

There is a persistent problem of language in population. Some countries that argue against "family planning" have in fact services for lowering fertility far exceeding those of others who have just begun to adopt official programmes under this label. There is confusion because the objectors to "family planning" use some other terms like "birth control", "birth spacing", "family health services", "responsible parenthood", "maternal and child health services", or "family welfare services". Since the objection is not on the grounds of practice which is similar, clearly it must be on the ideological or political connotations of the term "family planning". One significant gap in the Bucharest conclusions was the failure to agree on a set of definitions to describe these practices in a politically neutral manner that could be adopted universally by those interested in population programmes.

I see it a part of the Fund's duty to endeavour with the help of the other members of the United Nations system to work towards a generally acceptable technical population language that can be used for communication rather than confrontation.

One other post-Bucharest phenomenon has been the apparent reluctance in international meetings to talk about population as a key factor in development. In the recent Special Sessions of the United Nations on the New International Economic Order, almost all other issues that are globally important were subject to discussion—food, agriculture, industry, technology, international assistance, trade, and balance of payments problems, but population was conspicuously absent.

Was this omission due to the belief that there was nothing left to say about population? Or was there a belief that Bucharest had "solved" the population problem? Or was there a feeling that the still controversial subject of population might disturb attempts at consensus on the other major issues? I hope not.

If this reticence persists, I think it will be unfortunate. If one takes a broader view of economic problems and their causes, population cannot be neglected, especially so soon after the world community at Bucharest has emphasized the degree to which it was an integral factor in overall economic and social problems. At the end of 1975 the world population was estimated at around 4 billion and growing. Until some global balance is achieved, the consequences of too-rapid growth will continue to lead to crises in agriculture, industry, trade, and many other related areas. It is simply unrealistic to ignore an underlying cause of these difficulties. We cannot let periodic hunger and constant poverty in many parts of the world be our only reminders to put population problems on the agenda.

Even if international declarations do not solve problems, they usually encourage serious attempts to work them out.

Continuous discussion of population problems is needed, though at times rhetoric tends to retard rather than advance clear formulation of the issues. The Fund's experience in the past indicates that despite confused terminology and discontinuous dialogue, governments are undertaking population programmes not thought possible only a few years ago. Their realization of the importance of these programmes can be measured by the rising tide of requests coming to UNFPA.

The expansion of activities was made easier by the gradual acceptance among recipient governments that they could not hope for a universal panacea for solving population problems. It was best to start with a modest national programme than to wait for a global solution. As experience widened in most of these countries, they discovered that family planning practices from other countries usually could be adapted to their own cultural and political conditions. Most of these efforts are not sensational and will therefore never reach the newspaper headlines. But in the end it is these small unflagging exertions that count.

The Programmes Today

Reconciling the views of the donors and the recipients, as I have already pointed out, is a recurring problem in programming technical assistance. Putting together a programme which is globally acceptable has been an annual test for the Fund's professional and persuasive skills. We feel the outcome has been successful because we have been able to demonstrate to both sides that each part of the programme, no matter how views on it may differ, was a step towards the ultimate goal of achieving a balance between people and resources.

While countries in the developing world are all aware of population problems, they differ in their approach to them and in the degree of comprehensiveness of the measures which they take. In the South and East Asian countries, which were the first to act, most of the programmes are designed to lower fertility through family planning. In Africa and West Asia, where there has been a lack of basic population data, most of the programmes are for censuses, sample surveys, and related analyses. In

Latin America and the Caribbean there is a mix of both activities. Programmes usually show an early emphasis in collecting basic data followed by an increase in family planning and related programme activities. In all these regions there are efforts to orient population programmes within socioeconomic plans.

This is, of course, a very broad generalization. Population densities and other factors cause some governments to undertake programmes not typical of their regions. National population programmes do not follow a uniform series of stages from data collection to a comprehensive family planning programme. Each country's approach results from a complex set of circumstances. For instance, the approaches of Costa Rica and Tunisia to their population problems are of a kind more commonly found in Asia and the Pacific countries than in Latin America or Africa.

On Resources

Anticipating the demands that will be eventually made on the Fund, I warned as early as 1973 of a possible plateauing of our resources within a few years. The cumulative growth of UNFPA resources has been phenomenal—a hundredfold increase since 1969. But this has been matched by an equally phenomenal demand for assistance. The 1975 annual budget of $80 million barely covered bed-rock demand reached after much pruning of requests. All the indications are that requests will continue to skyrocket for some time to come.

Funding at the levels of activity we project means that we have to raise between $580 to $650 million in the four-year period 1976-9. This has been more than twice what we have raised so far. Our ability to obtain these amounts will depend on the acceptability of our future operations to the donor countries. As a rule, donor countries are liberal on their contributions if they are convinced of the urgency of the need as well as being satisfied with the delivery of programmes to the recipient countries.

I have previously described the effort that has gone into getting increased resources for the Fund and country programmes. Links to UNDP assistance and arrangements with bilateral aid programmes are examples of this effort. In particular, the fundraising effort in the oil-exporting countries will be doubly significant to us. It would mean that the developing countries which have the capacity to do so would be willing through multilateral assistance to help in this very vital programme in a way they have not done in the past.

While in the intermediate decades the volume of international assistance must increase as increasing demands indicate, I want to emphasize that the Fund does not envision asking for continuously increasing resources for ever. On the contrary, the total volume should gradually be restricted to just as much as necessary for the support of those country activities which for one or another reason still require international assistance and necessary global and regional activities which can only be carried out through international organizations. Therefore we are seeking a degree of commitment from recipient countries that they will finance population programmes mostly from their own resources, as they do in traditional areas like food production, education, and health services.

Programme Priorities

Filling the gap between resources and requests has also brought the question of priorities to the fore. The World Population Plan of Action failed to produce global priorities. Five regional consultations and one interregional meeting of experts since then did no better. Thus the Fund in its need to maintain the flow of resources to meet the requests has now to submit proposals for discussion in its governing bodies. Reaching consensus may take several sessions.

Under the lowest of our resource projects for 1976-9, the nature of the Fund's programme over the next several years would be largely determined by the components of the ongoing programme. Although the termination of projects would allow the acceptance of new requests, the existing composition of the programme would remain largely as it is, adjusting very slowly to countries' changing needs. Thus the Fund would continue to assist basic population data collection, family planning and maternal and child health, along with support services, population policy formulation and multi-sector activities.

The composition of the UNFPA programme will also depend on the magnitude of the funds available to UNFPA relative to demand. If resources are adequate to meet demand, substantial direct help can be given to many aspects of country programmes. If they do not reach this level, however, they will to a much larger extent have to be used as seed money for regional and global activities in such fields as training and research.

The recipient countries have understood from the start that however broadly UNFPA interpreted its mandate, it was a special purpose fund concerned with population. They have, therefore, sought to relate projects and programmes we were assisting to other broader elements of their economic and social development efforts. In most instances this was not hard to do. The demographic data we were helping them to collect was a necessary input to these programmes, and similarly family planning projects were usually a vital part of broader health measures. There is, however, much more for the Fund and other organizations to do in devising modes for integrating population programmes with those in agriculture, health, industry, employment—especially concerning women, and general rural development. These are the critical linkages for population programmes in the future.

In the long term, population efforts will have to focus in several key areas if the balance between people and resources is to be achieved:

The first of these is in the field of basic data collection. Eighteen countries still have not held censuses. Many more developing countries are in great need of vital statistics systems. The World Fertility Survey has to be completed—its contribution to population knowledge is eagerly awaited. Existing population data bases have to be updated and further refined. In this the United Nations system has been a key factor. Its support to countries must continue and intensify until universal reliability of data is achieved.

Secondly, work towards the development of an "ideal contraceptive" which is safe, effective, reversible, acceptable, and easy to administer must be continued. In this effort, the cooperation of countries and international organizations like World Health Organization is vital. Only a few countries today have the resource capacity to undertake this basic research. In the meantime the use of existing contraceptive methods must be encouraged in countries where they are acceptable.

Thirdly, there must be a more vigorous support for population training programmes initiated and conducted by developing countries. In substance the interdisciplinary approach must be encouraged to make these programmes effective. Equally important is the support to management programmes for better delivery of population services.

Fourthly, there must be a periodic reformulation of an international strategy to deal with population problems. National action is vital, but without a set of generally accepted guidelines, country efforts will fall short of making a significant contribution to an international drive to solve what in the end is a global problem.

Finally, population policy formulation and implementation must be further advanced by the individual countries. While governments are the ultimate judges of the direction and manner of national action and their consistency with national cultural values, it is vitally important that they think in terms of wider involvement of their peoples in population activities *now*. Time is an overriding factor and it is imperative that population programmes be implemented as efficiently and effectively as possible while there is still time to do so.

As We Move

By the turn of this century there will be almost seven billion humans on this planet. Where are governments to get the food, the clothing, the shelter, the medical service, and the educational facilities to take care of all these people?

I am not a believer in alarms. Nor, as an administrator, am I caught in the dilemma which immobilizes many, that "what can be done is not enough and what is enough cannot be done". I believe, on the contrary, that at any point much can be usefully done. The magnitude of this very human problem, however, makes me pause—many times. And, in reflection, I am firmly convinced that what is needed is not sudden gushes of enthusiasm, but a steady, patient, imaginative effort from the countries to solve their own problems as their particular situations demand.

There will probably be more crises like those in Bangladesh and the Sahel. I am certain there will be a continuing demand to humanize the technologies of our assistance before this century ends. Throughout all this we must devote unflagging attention to the underlying problems of which the crises are merely symptoms.

As I said in the beginning of this book, I was anxious to know whether or not the techniques of managing development programmes which I and my colleagues utilized in my country would have some validity in a multinational setting like the United Nations. They were, in essence, adaptations of what I had learned about the Western style of management with its requirements of objectivity, functional specificity, and efficiency, to my country's cultural demands for openness and its ideas on the importance of people and harmony. I have found that this synthesized approach was well suited to the international setting, and I have encouraged my colleagues in the Fund to adopt it. Today we feel gratified not simply because we have done a job but because collectively we have put together an organization that can work effectively within its environment. It could be a foundation upon which other administrators with different visions could build.

I also believe that there has been a timely beginning in the international community with the creation of UNFPA and its subsequent energizing of the other United Nations agencies and governments to assist in the solution of population problems. But this consciousness and these efforts to be globally effective must be done within a framework of an effective international organization.

Many changes are taking place in the United Nations system, the full implications of which are not yet apparent. New personalities have appeared in key positions in the United States system including Gabriel van Laethem, the Under Secretary-General for Economic and Social Affairs, who succeeded Philippe de Seynes; Bradford Morse, who took over the administration of the UNDP from Rudolph Peterson; and Edouard Saouma and Amadou-Mahtar M'Bow, who are now heading FAO and UNESCO respectively. Others will come to make their own personal and professional impact on the world organization and to give it a new look.

But in the final count the member governments of the United Nations will decide the future shape of what development assistance will be. The General Assembly will soon be in session to consider the restructuring of the United Nations system.

The proposals for restructuring are based on two very basic considerations which have the consensual understanding of the countries. First, that there must be a solution to the global maldistribution of income through peaceful and legitimate means. Second, that the modes of giving assistance must be aimed at developing self-reliance in the developing countries. Multilateral development assistance has basically taken the form of a transfer of technical knowledge and skills from the developed to the developing countries. It has been obvious for some time that after two decades of exchanges the developing countries have acquired sufficient expertise to make the original methods inadequate. These considerations, I feel as a developing country administrator, should shape future discussions on structure.

The Fund was fortunate to come into operation in the midst of these developments and thus to be in the enviable position of being able to innovate and depart from procedures for delivering assistance conceived two decades earlier. What we found highly effective was the fundamental policy of allowing recipient countries to determine policies and devise implementation procedures most suited to their needs. In the process we made several innovations. These included supporting local costs, utilizing more national institutions and experts, collaborating with non-governmental organizations outside the United Nations system, providing general budgetary support to ongoing government programmes, waiving requirements for counterpart funds, and encouraging direct implementation of programmes by countries themselves. These are the routes to self-reliance as we see it and a validation of the mutual trust and respect countries have for each other.

While population must be linked to development, it is my belief it should continue to be a distinct activity. Like housing, food, health, and environment, it will continue to be one of the major problems of man. The development structure of the United Nations that will foreseeably come about must take this into account just as in the internal management of the Fund it will be well to take note of what led to its growth and acceptance:

> To respond adequately to the demands of the developing countries and at the same time maintain the trust of our donors, we adopted programming policies of flexibility and neutrality;
>
> to be effective in the delivery of our assistance, we have been open, patient in listening, and quick to react to the directions given us by the countries;
>
> to be efficient, we have maintained one of the lowest administrative costs in the United Nations system and raised our implementation ratio to high levels;

to maintain our organizational integrity, we sought the cooperation of all the agencies and organizations doing business with us without being arbitrary in our decisions or demanding because we are the custodian of the resources;

to maintain a wholesome work environment, we have made participatory decision making a working principle within the organization and delegated much authority to responsible officers;

to encourage creativity, we have increased opportunities for the young and women to join us and attracted the energetic and the ambitious without being disconcerted with their presence;

to maintain order, we did not have to sterilize initiative nor confine officers to tight compartments.

Because we have decided to work for people and not numbers, I am confident that the Fund will be able to devise types of assistance and modes of delivery which will take fuller and fuller account of the dignity of the individuals and of his capacity for self-reliance and self-determination and at the same time help countries keep track of the global necessity to maintain a viable balance between people and resources.

The accomplishments of the Fund in the past six years have been due to the very large number of individuals that made it—some of whose names appear within the pages of this book. My own personal contribution has been the creation of an organizational environment in which talent was allowed to perform at its best. It was a wise Asian who once said: "Success is evident when everyone who helped in the task can say with conviction: 'I did it.' " And that is what I would like to have done here: help build an organization which has done the task assigned and is capable of doing its job for as long as there is need for it to do so.

Appendix I

Representatives of Governments and Organizations

H.E. A. E. Abdel Meguid (*Egypt*)
E. O. O. Aiyedun (*Nigeria*)
H.E. I. A. Akhund (*Pakistan*)
O. Aksoy (*Turkey*)
H.E. R. Alarcon Quesada (*Cuba*)
H.E. O. Algard (*Norway*)
G. M. Allagany (*Saudi Arabia*)
M. Y. Artan (*Somalia*)
H.E. S. M. Al Saffar (*Bahrain*)
S. Al-Shaikhly (*Iraq*)
H.E. H. S. Amerasinghe (*Sri Lanka*)
H. Amneus (*Sweden*)
R. K. Andresen (*Norway*)
A. L. Auguste (*Trinidad and Tobago*)
E. Bahr (*Fed. Rep. of Germany*)
A. C. Barnes (*USA*)
H.E. J. M. Baroody (*Saudi Arabia*)
D. E. Bell (*USA*)
H.E. A. Y. Bishara (*Kuwait*)
M. Bekele (*Ethiopia*)
M. Boserup (*Denmark*)
H.E. A. E. Boyd (*Panama*)
H.E. I. Boye (*Senegal*)
H.E. G. Bush (*USA*)
A. Chandrasekhar (*India*)
H.E. Chen Chu (*China*)
H.E. S. A. Consabir (*Venezuela*)
A. D. Cooper (*UK*)
H.E. I. Datcu (*Romania*)
H.E. L. de Guiringaud (*France*)
K. T. de Graft-Johnson (*Ghana*)
H.E. B. Dessande (*Chad*)
H.E. R. Driss (*Tunisia*)
S. Edzang (*Gabon*)
H.E. A. K. El Eryani (*Yemen Arab Republic*)

H.E. M. El Hassen (*Mauritania*)
H.E. M. Fall (*Senegal*)
U. Figueroa (*Cuba*)
A. Faraj (*Org. for African Unity*)
K. N. Freitas (*Togo*)
R. Gachter (*Switzerland*)
H.E. A. Garcia Robles (*Mexico*)
P. Gerin-Lajoie (*Canada*)
H.E. E. Ghorra (*Lebanon*)
H.E. C. Giambruno (*Uruguay*)
A. Goldschmidt (*USA*)
M. Green (*USA*)
S. D. Greene (*Liberia*)
H.E. K. M. Hagras (*Oman*)
J. Hannah (*USA*)
O. Harkavy (*USA*)
G. Harrar (*USA*)
J. Hartnack (*Denmark*)
J. Hart (*UK*)
K. Hedemann (*Norway*)
H.E. H. Hjorth-Nielsen (*Denmark*)
F. C. G. Hohler (*UK*)
D. Hopper (*Canada*)
M. W. Hosni (*Egypt*)
H.E. F. Hoveyda (*Iran*)
H.E. A. Humaidan (*UAE*)
H.E. A. H. Hussein (*Somalia*)
T. Iguchi (*Japan*)
H.E. J. Y. Jamal (*Qatar*)
H.E. M. Kanazawa (*Japan*)
H.E. A. Karhilo (*Finland*)
H.E. S. A. Karim (*Bangladesh*)
H. Kastoft (*Denmark*)
H.E. J. Kaufmann (*Netherlands*)
R. W. Kitchen, Jr. (*USA*)
H.E. M. R. Kikhia (*Libyan Arab Rep.*)

L. Klackenberg (*Sweden*)
J. H. Knowles (*USA*)
H.E. T. T. B. Koh (*Singapore*)
T. Kuroda (*Japan*)
S. Kuyama (*Japan*)
H.E. G. Lang (*Nicaragua*)
D. P. Lindores (*Canada*)
H.E. U Lwin (*Burma*)
A. Mahgoub (*Sudan*)
J. Maier (*USA*)
M. Majara (*Lesotho*)
Robert Martin (*Canada*)
T. Mamadou (*Org. of African Unity to UN*)
H.E. S. Marcuard (*Switzerland*)
W. Mathieson (*UK*)
H.E. M. Medani (*Sudan*)
J. Meijer (*Netherlands*)
H.E. D. O. Mills (*Jamaica*)
A. Mitra (*India*)
H. Moltrecht (*Fed. Rep. of Germany*)
A. M. Monyake (*Lesotho*)
H.E. D. P. Moynihan (*USA*)
H. Neufeldt (*Fed. Rep. of Germany*)
S. A. M. Ngallaba (*Tanzania*)
L. I. Nelson (*USA*)
A. Nsekaliji (*Rwanda*)
T. Ohtaka (*Japan*)
F. O. Okediji (*Nigeria*)
A. M. Oliveri-Lopez (*Argentina*)
J. Olver (*USA*)
D. Outtara (*Mali*)
H.E. A. Panyarachun (*Thailand*)
V. Prachuabmoh (*Thailand*)
H.E. S. F. Rae (*Canada*)
A. Ragai (*Syria*)
H.E. A. Rahal (*Algeria*)
H.E. N. G. Reyes (*Philippines*)
H.E. I. Richard (*UK*)

M. Rouge (*France*)
H.E. O. Rydbeck (*Sweden*)
H.E. S. Saito (*Japan*)
W. Sakrini (*Zaire*)
H.E. F. Salazar (*Costa Rica*)
H.E. I. Salifou (*Niger*)
H.E. C. Anwar Sani (*Indonesia*)
H.E. J. Scali (*USA*)
H. M. Schmid (*Fed. Rep. of Germany*)
H.E. S. Sen (*India*)
J. Shemirani (*Iran*)
G. W. Shroff (*New Zealand*)
G. Sigurdsen (*Sweden*)
O. M. Skoglund (*Sweden*)
H. Smith (*Canada*)
H.E. D. Slaoui (*Morocco*)
H.E. H. R. Tabor (*Denmark*)
T. Tanabe (*Japan*)
H.E. M. J. C. Templeton (*New Zealand*)
H.E. N. Terence (*Burundi*)
J. H. Thompson (*UK*)
Dr. Tiendraza (*Madagascar*)
C. van Tooren (*Netherlands*)
P. A. van Buuren (*Netherlands*)
C. Vigoa Llanes (*Cuba*)
W. Ulrichsen (*Denmark*)
H.E. J. Valdes (*Bolivia*)
D. J. van de Kaa (*Netherlands*)
L. van Gorkom (*Netherlands*)
S. Vervalke (*Belgium*)
H.E. R. von Wechmar (*Fed. Rep. of Germany*)
F. W. Walusiku (*Zambia*)
H.E. W. E. Waldron-Ramsey (*Barbados*)
D. Wright (*Canada*)
H.E. M. Yaguibou (*Upper Volta*)
H.E. H. M. A. Zakaria (*Malaysia*)

Appendix II

Former and Present UNFPA Professional Staff in Headquarters and the Field

T. Abrams
G. Adams
F. Ard
J. van Arendonk
F. Arkhurst
S. Aurelius
A. Aziz
Z. Aziz
B. Bantegui
G. Bartet
D. Bhatia
A. Bolaños
A. Burhanuddin
M. Carder (1974)[1]
C. Chandrasekaran (1974)
A. Chalkley (1973)
M. Cittone
J. Donayre
G. Duce
T. Eastwood
D. Ehrhardt
R. El Heneidi
S. Epstein
H. Fahmy
E. Ferguson
D. French (1975)
H. Gaenger
T. George (1975)
H. Gille
H. Goglio
A. Green

E. Gregory
I. Gudmundsson (1972)
A. Gythfeldt (1975)
A. Halliday (1973)
M. Hekmati
H. Hemmerich (1975)
I. Henkin
T. Kamihigashi (1975)
G. Kamwambe
J. Keppel (1975)
E. Kerner
A. M. Khan
M. Kotecha (1975)
A. Kusukawa
K. J. W. Lane
P. Lawrence (1975)
Y. Lee
N. Lenis
H. Lewis-Jones
V. Mack
G. Marcial (1974)
A. Marshall
S. Melchior
E. N. Meldahl
P. Micou
F. Mitchell
D. Moraes
L. N'Diaye
T. C. Nelson
M. O'Connor
L. Olivos

H. Ong
J. Ørner
P. Osinski
V. Peries
S. Raja Rao
S. Rhodes
G. Rolland
J. Sacklowski
N. Sadik
R. Salom
J. Santiago
A. P. Satterthwaite
C. H. Schaaf
T. Shuman
O. J. Sikes
J. Singh
S. L. Tan
A. Thavarajah
S. Tomita
E. Trainer
K. Trone
M. Vajrathon
W. Visser
T. Vittachi
J. Voelpel
H. Wagener
E. Wibmer
P. Witham
A. Zemanek
L. Zimmer (1974)

[1] Dates after name show when staff member left the employ of the Fund.

145

Name Index

147

Subject Index